Make a Beautiful Way

The Wisdom of Native American Women

∼

Edited by Barbara Alice Mann
Foreword by Winona LaDuke

University of Nebraska Press
Lincoln and London

Manufactured in the United States of America

∞

First Nebraska paperback printing: 2008

Library of Congress Cataloging-in-Publication Data
Daughters of mother earth.
Make a beautiful way: the wisdom of Native American women / edited by
Barbara Alice Mann; foreword by Winona LaDuke.
      p. cm.
Originally published: Daughters of mother earth: the wisdom of Native American women.
Westport, Conn.: Praeger, 2006. In series: Native America, 1552-8022
Includes bibliographical references and index.
ISBN 978-0-8032-6042-9 (pbk.: alk. paper)
1. Indian women—United States. 2. Matriarchy—United States. 3. Indians of North
America—Social life and customs. 4. Indians of North America—Public opinion.
5. Public opinion—United States. 6. United States—Social life and customs.
I. Mann, Barbara Alice, 1947– II. Title.
E98.W8D38 2008
305.48'897—dc22
2007048335

To the Seventh Generation

Contents

∽

Foreword

⁓

It is an interesting, terrifying, and promising time we find ourselves in. It is a new millennium, and Indigenous peoples, Indigenous women have survived five hundred years of destruction. We remain, changed by the process, transformed to survive, and on an Earth that is also transformed. It is the millennium in which we have experienced fifty years of a petroleum age, which although it arrived late in Indian country, has created a structural transition in our lives. With the advent of oil age and oil power, the power of labor, the power of growing food, the power of hands on the earth, has been largely replaced by the power of burning dinosaurs.

Thus, as Indigenous women today, we are also transformed, in that our thoughts are different; we think less about our food, our ways of surviving, and more about our place in a larger world than ever before. Although we always had and exercised the power of reflection, we have joined a dialogue, from which we were excluded for many centuries. Today, our voices, our experiences, remembered through our ancestors and through our lives today in the jackhammer of America, Canada, or elsewhere, are heard and seen.

The women and the stories here reflect that history, and the wonder of our times. As I read the chapters, I felt this life force of power entering my presence. Every Indigenous person has rankled and sickened at the omissions, stereotypes, and deception in a history written by a colonizer. The dehumanizing process is carried out through the words written, repeated, and branded upon a people, diminishing our stature as traditional people, as women, as a part of world history.

In challenging that dehumanizing process of writing colonial history, chains are removed and scar tissue can begin to heal. Moving through the experiences, the generations, and the traumas, putting voice and word to the history, and honoring our survival soothes a spirit which can be weary from the jackhammer. Redefining who we are today or beginning a dialogue from many varied perspectives elucidates the diversity that has been the vitality of life on earth. Biological diversity is essential for ecological sustainability, as is cultural diversity—we neither want an agricultural monocrop, nor a cultural monocrop—and, as Indigenous women, we are able to articulate the diversity of cultures, histories, and knowledges in Indigenous communities, reaffirming our own individual powers in the context of communities. That is how these voices and words reaffirm our potential in my eyes and thoughts.

In the reading of this work, I am drawn to all the voices, and find that my own voice and words hum in the larger women's song. In this millennium, where our peoples face the choices of alliance once again—an alliance with what our prophets would call the "scorched path" or what they would term "the green path"—I find that the discussions of remembering, deconstructing, recovering, and redefining in this book are essential to our choices and the recovery of our voices.

In the end, I am interested in deconstructing colonization, internal and external, and in the recovery of my own humanity. In that process, I see that the power is found to be who the Creator intended each of us to be as we walk on this earth, and that is how we will survive and make a beautiful way—*mino bimaatisiiwin*—for those who are yet to come and sing in this women's song.

Winona LaDuke
April, 2006

Preface

~

In that time before land on this water planet, so the Iroquoian elders say, the spirits of Earth noticed the Sky People passing by and thought to make them a little land proposition. Accordingly, all the elder spirits of Earth hurried up to a council in Sky World to suggest an infusion of Sky wisdom into Earth, thus to complete the Twinned Cosmos here by making dry land to complement the wet water.

Now, consensus does not require enthusiasm for a plan; it does not really even require investment in the idea. All it requires is a lack of dedicated opposition.

Generally, the elder spirits of Sky did not care much one way or the other whether land life began on Earth. They neither opposed nor championed the proposal, which the Earth spirits took as a consensual go-ahead. As they sprinted back home (before the spirits of Sky could reconsider), that White Panther, the Fire Dragon of Discord, the Meteor Man, zipped down with them, unnoticed.

The Fire Dragon of Discord has long made mischief on Turtle Island (North America), but he cannot stir up long-term trouble without human help. That is where the Europeans, those Salt Beings, came in handy, creeping in among the people, stripping away their rights, and grinding their children's faces into the dirt. One might think that these losses constituted the mischief, but one would be wrong.

The mischief surfaced later, in the twentieth century, as the children of Turtle Island began to stand up again, shake the dust from their clothing, and look about themselves. Squinting into the sun, they found that they did not recognize each other anymore. In fact, they did not even recognize themselves. Not only did they have a hard time just remembering what their elders had passed on to them, but worse, what they did recall seemed utterly commingled with what the Salt Beings brought.

Luckily, the elder spirits of Earth and Sky, Water and Air began speaking to the children again, telling them of the Old Things: that cooperation, not adversarialism, is the norm; that people are born perfect and must be fed poisons before they go sour; that the Grandmothers, not any government of men—and salty men at that—determine identity; that the Grandmothers properly direct society. They hear that clothing styles and fun make more powerful medicine than grim-faced prayer; that nurtured balance is the rule between men and women; that spirits of place must be respected; and that truth, however painful or shameful, is the best antidote to oppression.

For the duration of this book, the stirring sticks have been removed from the hands of the Fire Dragon of Discord as the Daughters of Mother Earth reclaim their ancient responsibility to speak in council, to tell the truth, to guide the rising generations through spirit-spoken wisdom. Paula Gunn Allen looks at Indian lifeways through the many stitches of their clothes and the many steps of their powwow fancy-dances. Lee Maracle calls for reconstitution of traditional social structures, based on Native American ways of knowing. Kay McGowan identifies the exact sites where woman-power was weakened historically through the heavy impositions of European culture, the better to repair them. Finally, I, Barbara Mann, examine how communication between Natives east and west of the Mississippi River became so deranged as to become dysfunctional and how to reestablish good east–west relations for the benefit of all our relations.

CHAPTER 1

Does Euro-Think Become Us?

~

Paula Gunn Allen

The Western world has had far more influence on how Native people think of ourselves than can be elucidated in a library large enough to fill one CD Rom with plenty left over. Under the category of *stereotypes*, at least 10,000 volumes could be shelved, and another 100,000 would be found under the general heading *revisionism*. In this chapter, I would like to add a small contribution to that longed-for, someday archive. My subject takes something from both the afore-mentioned headings, for stereotypes and revisionist views abound and not all come from non-Natives. Many of the areas of American culture that promote both stereotypes and revisionism have been addressed before, although the most frequently assaulted is the entertainment industry—whether in print or film, whether developed for children or adults. The next most often addressed are journalism and educational texts. Seldom is clothing ever mentioned, however.

Most of us are familiar with the common misconception of Indians as warring, buckskin-clad, poor-but-proud defenders of nature and her endless resources. Many of us remember the advertisement about litter, in which a Native actor duded up in "traditional" men's attire, long braids and all, gazed from the black-and-white spirit world to which all real Indians are, alas, consigned. A huge tear courses down his seamed cheek as he witnesses a meadow covered with trash: beer bottles, baby diapers, tin cans, and empty packages that held things like chips and cookies. A few paper plates are thrown in for dramatic effect. The scene then shifts to full color, with Euro-American children (not one Native kid among them), clean-faced and clear-eyed, dutifully picking up trash to deposit it in the appropriate receptacle.

Ah, see what our Native forefathers taught us? *Don't be a litterbug.*

I have yet to meet an Indian woman or man who is not offended by that commercial, even years after it stopped being aired. Not one of us can think of a time when *any* American institution was developed because of Native advice or weeping. Not one of us can think of one, danged thing that America has learned from what historian William Brandon has called "The Last Americans."[1]

Because of the image of the buckskin-wearing brave—or the even more elaborately buckskin-clothed chief crowned with the sine qua non of primal leadership (the eagle headdress replete with large, perfectly shaped feathers that trail down both sides nearly to the ground)—Americans and movie-goers of the world think that all Native people dress like that today, the few of us who are left, that is. "How quaint they are, how unique!"

For my part, I do not have to imagine strangers' ideas of us. They come right up to me and share them, inquiring innocently where they can go to see the once-proud denizens of a vanished landscape. Sometimes I burst out laughing while trying to respond respectfully, I am embarrassed to say. I laugh because I can see side-by-sides, as though on a split screen. What they are picturing, on the first screen, is Enviro-Indian, He of the Buckskin-Eagle Clan. Next to that is the second screen, the Pissed-Off Indian, beloved of cultural revisionists and leftist activists worldwide. The third, the one I am concerned with in this chapter as in my own life, is the Real-World Indian, who is largely invisible to those who live outside the framework of stereotypes. Outsiders cannot make out the image there because the clothing is all modern. I suppose it is better that I laugh over this rather than yell and throw insults. My ancestors would never recover from the shame if I did such a disreputable thing.

Still, so powerful are the images beamed at us via the great American network of all media—including the meme network of the sociopsychological—that most nonindigenous Americans think that all Indians were as the movies have us. Some older Americans, or Americans more addicted to reading novels from different eras, might add those buckskin-clad folks from farther east than the Plains—from Virginia, say, or maybe Connecticut. If we read our "dime novels" (a dime being about what popular novels cost in the early nineteenth century when "Indian" stories were an East Coast phenomenon), we would know that the braves had shaven heads with only a topknot from which hung a single feather, or at most two. Some male leaders wore an attenuated war bonnet that sat on the head much as a European monarch's metal crown sat and was about the same size in circumference. They might even know that female leaders wore turbans with very long tails made from a cloth about the size of a bed sheet, usually red and not infrequently flannel. Those handy tails could double as impromptu baskets.

In the Southwest, the Pueblos grew cotton, made it into yarn, and then wove it into clothing long before the Spaniards and hundreds of years before the English came. I have yet to see any mention of Southwestern Natives dressed in cotton in any other than specialized ethnographic studies, although the typical "Navajo" weavings that are used as rugs, horse blankets, and tapestries abound in contemporary American ideas of Southwestern style. By the same token, whereas the geometric patterns that characteristically pass as Indian or Native American designs are readily found on linens, outerwear, dresses, women's blouses, and skirts, the beautiful flower designs found all over Indian Country, from Wisconsin to the Atlantic seaboard, are as yet undiscovered by boutiques and merchandisers of ethnica.

Turbans or flowered cotton blouses like Mantas and utyinats are not for sale in "Indian" stores because the Plains-based stereotype dominates the market (for which, no doubt, Pueblos are grateful). However, Native nations' preferences are not an issue for marketers. For them, the sale is the thing, and because everyone knows what "real" Indians wear— buckskin and feathers, or some horrifying artificial version of them— they are usually what is for sale! Since racism has gained a bad name, the marketing images of what are commonly called "ethnic groups" fixate on the food or the dress of the target group. While "Middle Eastern," Chinese, Japanese, Thai, Italian, Ethiopian, East Indian, African American, and "Mexican" meals are readily available just about everywhere, American Indian foodstuffs—corn, beans, squash, tomatoes, potatoes—are never sold as Native American cuisine. Consequently, modern Indians get stuck with dressing the part. Across Turtle Island, Natives are bludgeoned with alien images of how we "should" look.

Sometimes we refuse to cooperate. It is not unusual for us to be asked to attend events in our "traditional" garb. Sometimes our responses are educational in nature. To kick off one such event, a multicultural celebration at a Midwestern university in the late 1990s, foreign students were invited to march into the assembly hall, all gussied up in their national attire and carrying their country's flag. Shawn Koons, a law student (then head of the Native American Student Association of the university), was asked not just to march in the "colorful" procession (of *foreigners*) but also to lead off the march. He marched all right in a red beret, an old T-shirt, tattered blue jeans, and worn-out sneakers. Flapping before him, he carried a white flag on a stick. Although Koons's antic was not much appreciated by the university administration, his point was on target.

For the most part, Native American men, women, and children dress much as everyone in their area dresses. In rural New Mexico, where I was raised, that usually means Levis, T-shirts, sweatshirts, Western shirts, and baseball caps, straw hats, or felt Stetsons. Although any who are mending fences (literally), herding cows or sheep, or traveling where only SUVs of the Hummer class can roam still ride horseback, Indian people typically drive automotive vehicles. These might be pickups, two-ton trucks, or SUVs for rural people who engage in ranching or similar occupations, or they might be a variety of cars, many of Japanese extraction. The cars are driven by urban and suburban Indians, as well as by many who live in rural areas but are employed in the health, education, law, accounting, writing, painting, filmmaking, journalism, politicking, and such fields. The parking lots at any good powwow will offer the observer quite a range of vehicles to view, and the brilliance of the regalia worn by the dancers, male and female, child and adult, will lead any attendee front-loaded by images of media Indians to be hard put to recognize the engineers, hackers, pilots, and business people out there on the floor.

Come to think of it, powwows are a good platform from which to view the more colorful side of contemporary Native America, as well as being a great source of fry bread and Navajo tacos. Every powwow begins with an opening prayer, and it is always Christian. The first dances, before the Grand Entry, are more "traditional" (although after four to five hundred years of Christianization, I suppose Christianity is as traditional an Indian identity as more preconquest parameters are). My favorite is the Gourd Dance, a Kiowa tradition that originated with the Kiowa Gourd Clan, a warrior society.

> When the Kiowa gathered for the K'aw-tow (literally "gathering"), they came together to build the K'aw-tow lodge, where the dancing would take place. These structures were built of large cottonwood trees and then covered with brush. The Brush Dance commemorated this act of building. Today, Brush Dances are often performed before Gourd Dances at annual celebrations. The very same songs are often sung in the Gourd Dance throughout the rest of the year. Many Brush Dance songs that have words reference the flirting and courting that occurred during the building of the K'aw-tow lodge. This "song with words" translates thus:

> > *Like somebody said,*
> > *That's the way it is,*
> > *I sure like to fall in love.*[2]

Intertribal Gourd Dance societies host Gourd Dances prior to most powwows. Most of the dancers are ex-servicemen and veterans of the last three wars. A gourd dancer's distinctive dance clothes consist of a red and blue blanket draped over the shoulders so that both ends hang in front, a woven sash at the waist, and bandoliers of mesquite beans or large cut glass beads worn over street clothes. In their right hands, dancers shake rattles made of gourds or German silver canisters. In their left, they hold loose feathers or eagle fans. Beadwork is usually of the fine-cut bead variety associated with peyote ceremonies. Singers stand and hold the drum above the ground or use hand drums. For the Gourd Dance, which is held before the Grand Entry and the powwow proper, women wear shawls and dance at the outer edge of the circle, whereas men dance in a stationary position, lifting their heels off the ground in beat to the drum. They dance slowly, keeping time with their rattles.[3]

The powwow officially begins with the Grand Entry, headed by the Head Man and the Head Woman, mature or elderly people of stature in the community. They are closely followed by flag-bearers, who carry both the Stars and Stripes and the state flag of whatever state the dance is being held in. They might also carry the tribal banner of the host Native tribe or nation. All of those who will participate in the dancing enter during this time. At some of the larger powwows, there can be several hundred dancers, entering the dance ground in pairs.

The dances that follow are almost all of the Plains variety, and the drums—there may be as many as seven or eight—are identified as either Northern or Southern Plains. Each drum is a very large one, as much as five feet in diameter. Around each drum, seven or so men sit on folding chairs, one drumstick in each man's hand. These are about a foot long, the business end made of stuffed buckskin lashed onto the drumstick with a rawhide strip. The singers' styles, as well as their repertoire, are distinct; the Northern singers sing at the high end of the register, whereas the Southern singers stay within a more moderate range.

For the most part, the men are dressed in Plains-style regalia: roach on head, bustle made of a hoop of large feathers, loincloth usually worn over jeans (sometimes shorts), beaded moccasins, and a cuff on each ankle of large tin bells, making a sound like Christmas. They hold a fan made of wing feathers (and perhaps another item in the other hand) and wear beaded bands on their biceps. The younger men, and many older ones as well, do something called "the Men's Fancy Dance," a routine that is about quick movements of feet, raised knees, bent backs, and bobbing heads. The best look as much like great birds as human men, and when they are at their best, there is little as breath-takingly beautiful in the human world.

Meanwhile, the women—along with children and many older men—move at a more leisurely pace around the circle. Beyond the inner circle, most of the men, as well as young women who engage in fancy dancing, dance outside the women's circle so they can move freely without crashing into our more sedate, dignified selves. Attired variously, depending on region of the country and tribal affiliation, the women all wear beautiful shawls. The work on them and the beadwork on their armbands, leggings, and moccasins is ever more stunning. Many women dress in their own traditional dress, for the most part variations on the "Mother Hubbard" dress foisted on Native women from sea to shining sea by missionaries who thought that clothes make the person human. (Euro-Americans were always more interested in appearance than character it seems, perhaps because in such a diverse society as America was by the mid-nineteenth century, there were few other ways to signal belonging and thus improve one's chances of survival.) It is horrifyingly true that differences in dress alone could lead to early and bloody extirpation for men women and children.

This was doubly true of dress-offenders who were Native peoples. Anyone who thinks that the slaughter of innocents—at what is known as "The Great Swamp Fight" (1675) in what is now Rhode Island, Goschochking (1782) in what is now Ohio, Sand Creek (1864) in what is now Colorado, or Wounded Knee (1892) in modern-day South Dakota—was horrifying should study the conquest of California during and just after the Gold Rush for tales of true terrorism, worse even than the Long Walk of the Diné or the Cherokee Trail of Tears. Probably most telling was that the California murders were proudly published in local papers. The *Sacramento Bee* of the mid-nineteenth century is a major source of back-slapping tales of slaughter. The coastal Indians, by the way, did not have (and still do not, except in English or Spanish) a word for *argument*, never mind for *warfare*. It seems they are as conflict-phobic as the Pueblos of the American Southwest. So much for the brave warrior tradition. It wasn't the brave warrior, after all, who lost the country. To quote the late U.S. Senator S. I. Haiakawa of California, in a slightly more limited reference, "[The United States] stole it fair and square." The scariest part of these long-denied tales of terrorism is that what goes around, comes around.

That being said, one of the positive developments to come out of this dreadful past is the clothing, which, like Indian humor, is based in tradition but fits with the new circumstances in which we find ourselves. The history of what is now considered "traditional" dress is instructive. Each clan and nation's women adapted the original plain, poor white woman's dress (usually made of gingham) in ways similar to the way, a thousand years earlier, the Japanese adapted Chinese-imposed cultural "norms" to a Japanese style—even including the religion, Buddhism. Losing nothing of significance in the process, the now-traditional dress of the Cherokees or the Salish, the Apaches or the Pueblos are unique to each group's aesthetic and historic sensibilities. One might comment that necessity is not only the mother of invention but also of creativity itself.

Our present-day traditional women's dress features a boxy version of the original dress. It is one piece and features three-quarter-length sleeves that end in a three- or four-inch, slightly gathered ruffle. The bottom of the dress is similarly finished. At the place where the ruffles join the body of the garment, rickrack of matching colors is sewn. The underdress, usually print, is thus accented. Over this basic underdress is the traditional manta, a straight piece of fabric that is fashioned so that one edge fits over the shoulder while the other goes under the other arm. Which side is up is significant. Once, I put mine on backward and my grandmother chided me. "Put it on the right shoulder," she said. "Wearing it on the left shoulder means you're dead!"

The Northwest adaptation is one of my favorites. The Mother Hubbard became the "jingle dress," so known because the dresses—which feature mid-length wide sleeves that drape over the arm to just below the elbow—are studded throughout their free-hanging length with tiny cowrie shells or small cone-shaped bells that make a jingle sound. Like the men, women dancers also carry fans fashioned from bird wings. They are mounted on a handle of polished wood and are quite handsome. Women also wear powwow bags, purses about five by seven inches that hang from a length of twisted silk twine. Often made of very soft buckskin, like the moccasins, they display beadwork of great finesse and beauty. My favorite design for both is a large pink, green-leafed rose in opalescent glass beads. Those who define such items as "crafts" do not know the meaning of "art."

Around the powwow dance proper, the drums are arranged. Beyond them, dancers and their families set up lawn chairs where they can spread out their blankets and other gear: baby strollers, babies, and the like. Somewhere in this area, the MC stand will be erected; from there, the dances will be announced and opening and closing prayers offered. Most of the powwows are opened with some appeal to God, in the Christian sense, often by a local Indian minister or the Master of Ceremonies.

Although I have heard several accounts of the origins of powwows, I can say that the word was profoundly connected to the identity of those Algonquin tribes participating in the Powhatan Alliance in the area first claimed by the English at James Fort (later known and valorized as Jamestown). The Powhatan, a loosely allied group of Southern Algonquin-speaking communities or tribes, took the name from a concept central to their way of life and consciousness.

We modern people are matter-based and pride ourselves on our ability as individuals and nations to reason. Algonquins in general and Powhatans in particular were spirit-centered and prided themselves as a group on their ability stay connected while awake, going about their daily tasks in touch with the nonmaterial world, the one called *dream* in English. *Powhatan* means "People of the Dream" and *powwow* means "let us dream together." The term got carried West by Americans during the nineteenth century's great westward movement. It was taken to signify "meeting" or "gathering" and is in use today particularly in politics or when leaders in business or other enterprises convene to set policy and strategize.

Modern powwows themselves are evidently Plains in origin; a tradition for perhaps a century, since Haskell Indian School was opened in Kansas. Indian graduates from all over the territory—from the Dakotas to New Mexico, as well as from Ohio, perhaps even farther east and west—would meet every few years for a reunion. I remember that my mother's uncles (John, Wallace, and I suppose, Bruce—who lived in Idaho, so I am not certain about him), graduates all, would head for Haskell. According to accounts I read by Indian scholars interested in powwow history, those gathered for the reunion would enjoy "traditional" dances, meaning those traditional to northern and (I guess) southern Plains nations.

My uncles, of course, were Laguna Pueblo; however the Indian boarding school phenomenon began a move toward a kind of pan-Indian identity that has served us in all kinds of venues during the twentieth century and, so far, in the twenty-first as well. It is certain that, by their intertribal nature, Haskell and other Indian schools that took in children from various nations fostered a fair amount of intertribal marriage. The descendents of such matches were often twice-blessed: They got two sets of languages, customs, traditions, and styles of cooking, dressing, and singing. Of course, they also got two sets of responsibilities and fewer rights. (In traditional generalities, Indians do not have "rights"; we have *responsibilities* and proper ways in which we fit into and contribute to the community. This is not to say that Native people should therefore eschew the constitutionally granted "rights" enjoyed by all American citizens, only that we have a strong tendency to think of responsibilities long before we think of rights, even those who are raised far from the traditions and their homelands.[4])

All the Indian boarding schools were dedicated to the express purpose of "taking the Indian out of the child" (cultural genocide), which American liberals such as Thomas Jefferson preferred to the other option (physical genocide). The government schools had another, probably unintended consequence, however. The earliest (after the one at Henrico, a few miles upriver from James Fort) was Carlisle. My great-grandmother was one of the earliest attendees there. Like Pocahontas, she married a white man, albeit a Scots American from Ohio named Kenneth Colin Campbell Gunn, who had come with his brothers to Laguna while surveying for the railroad. Although I doubt that eradicating culture included marrying out in the power brokers' plans, my colleague and the editor of this volume informs me that "marrying out was specifically promoted as cultural genocide by an 1888 U.S. law, 25 Stat. L, 392, connected with the Dawes Act. Women marrying out specifically lost their Native identity, and so did all children of the marriage." However, that was not true for the Lagunas, nor for other Pueblos. Although my great-grandmother married out, neither she, her children, nor her grandchildren were considered non-members of the Laguna tribe. This just goes to show how out of touch with the United States New Mexico has long been.

In the 1960s or 1970s, when Santa Clara Pueblo denied artist Helen Harding Pueblo status because her mother married out, Harding sued. The U.S. Senate and later the House passed an Indian Civil Rights Act of sorts that acted effectively as a guarantee of tribal rights to children and grandchildren of tribal members. Santa Clara was and is a tribe that tracks tribal and clan membership via the father's line; the Keres Pueblos, including the Laguna, are mother-right systems that track clan and tribal membership via the mother's line. Nowadays, for purposes related to U.S. rules and regulations, Pueblos officially track heritage via either parent.

Back to powwows, the significant point is that they, like the movie and teleland Indians, are THE PLAINS TYPE. The dominant, media-fed Indian stereotype is Sioux, mainly Lakota. Even the agricultural Sioux, who live where they did for centuries before the great move across the Missouri onto the Great Plains in the late nineteenth century, are ignored. Exactly why the buffalo-and-Sun Dance Sioux are the iconic Indians remains unclear. The origin of this stereotype might lie in one of the earliest Westerns made in Hollywood, *Custer's Last Stand* (1936). The film might have found its way into the same, naive national consciousness that the mostly bogus tales of the Old West helped create. As a historical aside, Ronald Reagan's first major movie role was as Custer in one of the earliest Last-Stand movies, *The Santa Fe Trail* (1940). Moreover, the first film ever made for the big screen was *Custer's Last Stand* (1909).

In any case, from Custer's defeat at the Little Bighorn to a fictional Civil War officer observed by wolves dancing alone on the empty plains in *Dances with Wolves* (1990), it seems that the buffalo head nickel does not depict the only Indian Americans ever loved. The brave warrior who melts off into the haze of romance, American style, holds at least second place. That these icons of days gone by say more about the American psyche than about American Indians is obvious. They speak both to the American dream, which is all about freedom based on financial independence, and war, which is all about protecting that freedom. That neither had anything to do with the settlement of Europeans and others all over the continent—nay, the whole hemisphere— is a carefully nurtured falsehood.

Furthermore, exactly why the dominant Indian image in Indian Country is, from coast to coast, the Plains-style dance gathering known as the powwow is even more obscure. Aside from the Haskell connection and the fact that Indians are after all also Americans, I can think of only one reason that Indians themselves hold this same stereotype: their investment in the U.S. military, an investment long supported and reinforced by compulsory attendance at the Indian Boarding Schools, run by the U.S. Department of War. Only later, when the Department of War became the Department of Defense, was the operation of these schools transferred to the Bureau of Indian Services under the Department of the Interior.

Even today when the curriculum at Indian Schools has changed dramatically and attendance at them is no longer compulsory, Native men and women enlist in the U.S. armed forces at a greater percentage per capita than any other group. Although this is at least partially attributable to boarding school education, where boys were trained in a military style, it also seems to be an equally strong tradition among those very Indians of the western Midwest famed for their prowess in wartime. Never mind that the traditional kind of war in which those same people engaged did not include the death of the adversary. Although the engagements did take great courage, "counting coup" was more a matter of putting the adversary to shame before his peers than of slaughtering one another. It seems that, for true warriors, being bested was so hard to endure that death might have been preferable. However, it would not have provided the victor with the spiritual power that his success would garner.

Although the intent and expression of Native warfare differs from the modern American thrust in both style and scope, D'Arcy McNickle, Native historian and Pulitzer Prize winner, tells us that fully 70 percent of all Native nations were essentially pacifist. However, under the new exigencies required by the imposition of U.S. governmental "norms" on peoples for whom war was far from the norm, enlistment in the U.S. armed forces perhaps functions as a sort of meeting ground for modern Indians of all nations. After their military stints, one way to continue meeting is through the powwow, just about the only social milieu for Native people in existence throughout the greater part of the twentieth century. Over the years since they became widespread, attendance has increased exponentially. There are some dancers who earn their livelihood traveling powwow to powwow, winning cash prizes that can be substantial, depending on the size of the gathering.

I was in my mid-thirties, living in San Francisco and teaching at San Francisco State University in the American Indian Studies program, when I attended my first powwow. My mother's youngest brother, Sidney, whom we knew as "Ook" or "Uncle Ookie," had moved there around the time I did, both of us joining my eldest sister, who had been living there for some time. Ook mentioned that there was a powwow in San Jose. When I asked him about it, he invited me to accompany him. Now that I think about it, since my great-uncles (Ook's uncles) had attended Haskell, including most of its reunions, one would think I would have heard about powwows before moving to urban coastal California! However, I had not.

Ook told me to take a shawl. I had one because my father's general merchandise store, the Cubero Trading Company in Cubero, New Mexico, where I was raised, sold them. I had gotten one the last time I was home, so on a bright July morning, we headed south on the Nimitz Freeway, my uncle all decked out in "ice cream" pants (white jeans), Navajo moccasins, and a blue velveteen Navajo-style shirt, a Pueblo woven belt around his middle. He had his hair done in a traditional Pueblo men's way, minus the bangs and side hair cut short to hang straight down from center part to the earlobe on each side. This meant that his long hair was twisted and then shaped into a figure-eight coil that rested at the nape of his neck. Wrapped around his head was a red scarf folded in the traditional manner. On the back seat, he placed his neatly folded Hudson's Bay blanket; he would wear it folded in thirds over his right arm when he danced.

This first powwow experience was pure culture shock. A commonly held misconception about sacred rituals in Indian Country is that they are always circular. This is usually mentioned as an example of how spiritual the Indians are as compared to the benighted Anglo-Europeans, who worship in rectangles and squares. Alas, we benighted Lagunas do not dance around in a circle but in lines that go back and forth across a rectangular center place. Not only are Pueblo dances linear and rectangular, but Navajo and Pueblo designs on weaving or pottery are also angular, geometric.

When something circular shows up for us, it is either a cloudhead, the head, or the face of a supernatural or a human. Where the circular style is prominent is on the Plains; the winds there sweep across thousands of miles of flatland. Their pattern is mostly circular, a *powa* (nonphysical power) that is at its greatest during "tornadoes." (Think of them as nonhuman people—Persons, as some old timers refer to them, or Holy People as the Navajo word *Yei* translates.) On the Great Plains, circularity is to be revered; the tornadoes are proof of that. In the eastern Rockies, circular patterns are eclipsed by linear or multifaceted geometric ones.

As major Persons have rectangular shapes around them, our home dance ground—which is blessed—is a place of non-physical power, or *powa*. It is bounded on each side by a multifamily, multistory building, each the home place of certain clans. Two of these structures are "summer people's" centers and two are "winter people's." The entries are not at the cardinal directions but at the lateral directions: northeast, northwest, southwest, southeast.

Consequently, the San Jose powwow was the first dance done in a circle that I had ever seen. Neither had I ever seen fancy dances, women's dances, a huge drum played by several men, or any of the Plains-style garb they wore (other than shawls, which Pueblo ladies wear in common with our Native sisters across Indian Country). That powwow, one of the early ones, did not feature many drums or hundreds of astonishingly beautifully garbed participants. Most of us were in jeans or dresses, and even the men who had bustles and headpieces wore them over their jeans and shirts. Many wore tennis shoes in lieu of moccasins. There was frybread, however, maybe the first I had tasted that went by that name. (My grandmother made frybread, but called it *sopapaillas*. Ook, of course, called it "sofapillows.") We got some fresh corn on the cob, the best I had tasted since I was a youngster. It was really fresh, homegrown I suppose, and this at a time when growing one's own food was not fashionable.

As the years passed and the powwow became big business in Indian Country, coast to coast and border to border, the attendance sky-rocketed, the booth population grew, and the regalia became ever more beautiful. So caught up in the romance and splendor of it all was I, that I noticed only recently that powwows, like the American Indian Movement and Hollywood Indians, were all Plains and heavily Lakota Sioux-influenced. It was not that the omnipresence of Lakota imagery had been lost on us Indians of other persuasions. At powwows and conferences, people from Indian nations all around the United States can usually be heard muttering, "We're not like that"; "We never ate buffalo"; or "Sheesh, those Lakota. They think they're the only true Indians!"

The degree to which the American media's image of Indians as warlike people who had been defeated in a just war and alas died out (being primitive and all) has impacted Indian self-awareness at very deep levels. It dominates Indian as well as non-Indian conceptions of *Indianismo*, despite the great differences between what we see in films and on television and what we see at home. The powwow is glamorous, after all; it is a great social setting for young people to find dates and for older ones to form new connections or sustain old ones.

The popular powwow serves many functions; among them is the four- or five-centuries-old, powerful subtext of the noble savage. In liberal and activist circles, this image is contextualized in such a way that said noble savage, though romantic and tragic, is hostile still, but righteously so. For many Americans (and Europeans for that matter), the Indian is the keeper of ecosanity and true spirituality. The idea is that "The Indian" is the wronged victim of out-of-control capitalism, imperialism, or general "whitism," to coin a phrase. That idea forms most public discussions of contemporary Indian life. So powerful is this image, however unreal, that only those Native people or ideas that conform to this view are touted in media of various kinds.

The most recent case in point is the National Museum of the American Indian located on Capitol Mall in Washington, DC. When it opened at the autumnal equinox, September 21, 2002, the early reviews in major newspapers reflected outrage. It seems that the Native people—who sent articles and advice on how to mount the exhibits and who served on the committees that finalized the opening exhibits—did not take into account either the notions of ethnographers or archeologists, nor did they pay much attention to the theme dear to the hearts of left-wingers and liberals alike: genocide.

The Wall Street Journal's op-ed piece framed the argument that viewers needed cards telling them what they were looking at. It was not only the name of the object that was wanted, but also how it was defined and what it was used for. It seems that ordinary Americans and visitors from around the globe are unable to identify pottery, bows and arrows, or various implements of food preparation, such as flint knives, cooking pots, and storage containers. Neither are they able to identify the richly varied display of clothing and personal ornaments without expert commentary to guide them. The editorial opinion seemed to me to speak more to the failures of media and educational institutions than to those of the Native exhibitors. The other complaint—voiced in the progressive media including one broadcast by National Public Radio and *Democracy Now!*, on which I appeared—was about the absence of exhibits detailing the conquest, all 500 years of it. In this view, what mattered was how rotten the Europeans, and later the United States, had been and are.

Evidently, what does *not* matter here is what the Native people want or how the numerous communities all over the Western Hemisphere perceive our own history and contemporary life. Indeed, self-definition, like self-determination and sovereignty, are required to follow clearly delineated lines set forth in the dictates of Euro-think. The *Wall Street Journal*'s ethnographic frame reflects a worldview that is only comfortable with the "facts," as defined by academically established experts and disciplines. The NPR frame reflects a worldview that, for its part, is comfortable only with pointing fingers at the Alpha Dogs of Europe and the United States. That Natives regard the European intrusion as but a fraction of our ancient experience, which we extend back to creation, got lost in the ruckus.

I do not mean to suggest that readers must disapprove of either approach; my point here is to highlight the extent to which varieties of the Euro-American worldview affect thinking about who we Indians are and of what our past consists. The ethnographic idea tells how much Indians are defined by academic disciplines that have much more to do with European than with indigenous thought. The left-wing political argument tells how we are defined by the left as victims of a rapacious capitalist establishment, with the foremost proponent of this deplored establishment being the United States.

There are frailties in both views. To begin with, academic disciplines are just that. They are not meant to define but to explore, in an ordered way, varieties of phenomena that arise in human consciousness and our world. The political stance, however, is the most troubling because it has direct and devastating consequences for everyone who lives in Indian Country, for Native people are, if anything, about as apolitical as anyone can get, at least in the Western sense. That is, we do not engage in polarizing arguments about which political stream is right and which is wrong. People vote, and, for the most part, that is the end of it. Many vote Republican, and many vote Democrat. A sizable number do not vote. As far as I know, only the Diné, the Navajo nation, urges its citizens to vote as a bloc, and this is done to pursue specifically Navajo concerns with state and federal policies that can determine, in large part, the quality of life for Navajo people both off and on the reservation.

The apolitical stance common to most tribal Americans reflects the same view of ourselves as the museum in Washington. We define ourselves; we identify with our communities and our traditions. They are both, for the most part, at least a thousand years old. One does not discard them as readily as one might a used pair of shoes. As it happens, Indians *are* the land, and that land is far older than the United States or the Eastern Hemispheric civilization from which it sprang.

Our communities may reflect their modern existence; communities do that—adjust themselves to the situation. Were they to fail in that adjustment, no one would be left to tell the tale. Assuredly, there are millions of us, ready and able to live in accordance with ancient tenets of respect for all living things, harmony, integrity, and wholeness. Certainly, doing so is not easy in this particular time and place; then again, perhaps "easy" is not the point. Maybe it is just because it is *not* easy that it is right and proper to do so. The Old Ones tell us, via the traditions and their example, that a life devoid of challenge is a life wasted. The human spirit grows toward maturity in the face of obstacles, not in the face of comfortable circumstances. Personally, I hate the facts of the matter; I like living in relative comfort, having at hand running water, electricity, instant heat, indoor cooking, bathing, and facilities for the release of bodily waste.

However, our outward circumstances have obviously changed. Whereas once we had literally eliminated poverty, American Indian communities are now among the most destitute groups in the wealthiest nation the world has ever seen. That more Indian people live below the poverty line than above it is a dreadful fact and one that cries out for redress. Still, raging and causing deep divisions among the very people who already do more than their share of suffering in the material sense is hardly a solution. Indeed, it is counterindicated in the context of indigenous consciousness, which has those same millennia behind it now guiding its most recent expression in the protocols, as established by the Indigenous People's Conference in 2002. The protocols were what I said: harmony, integrity, respect for all living things, and wholeness. The protocols sum up *hozho*, a Navajo word that means more or less what the protocols call for.

Those who believe that the word *squaw* (the Algonquin word for woman among many Algonquin peoples) must be deleted from any lexicon touched off quite a discussion about whose language it is anyway. At a Women's Studies Conference at Connecticut State University in October 2001, the plenary session addressed the issue directly. Abenaki (Algonquin) scholar and writer Marge Bruchac made the point that the word has long been a quite respectable word among various Algonquin dialects and simply meant "woman." In her essay "Reclaiming the Word 'Squaw' in the Name of the Ancestors," Bruchac instructs us first that "Squaw is not an English word." In the first subheading, she assures us that "Squaw means the totality of being female." Providing linguistic contextualizaton, she continues,

> It *is* a phoenetic rendering of an Algonkian word, or morpheme, that does *not* translate to mean any particular part of a woman's anatomy. Within the entire Algonkian family of languages, the root or morpheme, variously spelled "squa," "skwa," "esqua," "kwe," "squeh," "kw" etc. is used to indicate "female," not "female reproductive parts." Variants of the word are still in widespread use among northeastern peoples. Native speakers of Wabanaki languages use "nidobaskwa," to indicate a female friend, or "awassoskwa," to refer to a female bear; Nipmuc and Narragansett elders use the English form "squaw" in telling traditional stories about women's activities or medicinal plants; when Abenaki people sing the "Birth Song," they address "nuncksquassis," the "little woman baby." The Wampanoag people, who are in the midst of an extensive language reclamation project, affirm that there is no insult, and no implication of a definition referring to female anatomy, in any of the original Algonkian forms of the word.[5]

Alas, for some, scholarship such as Bruchac's is a red flag. Defying the protocols, the old ways, and much else besides rage, many indulge themselves in pelting Indians who provide objective information with hate mail, which, of course, is my point. Although the battle between the good and the evil, the right and the wrong, the light and the dark is profoundly captivating, said battle is also profoundly Eastern Hemisphere, Indo-Germanic, and, I might add, masculine. After all, the concept of conflict as the central organizing principal of human concourse derives directly from the ancient world's heroic epic tradition, which were within the province of men's storytelling. (Women's storytelling traditions were quite different; those I've seen bear a startling resemblance to stories from North American traditions that I have heard or read.)

In "The Lasting of the Mohegans: The Story of the Wolf People," Mohegan tribal historian Melissa Fawcett (who retook her family name, Tantaquidgeon, in 2002) puts the subject in a Mohegan (Algonquin) linguistic setting:

> Red is the color of women and life.... The Mohegan word for woman is "shquaaw" and red is "squayoh" Blood is referred to as "(um)sque" which also has a related "squ" root. [As does] the name of Granny Squannit,

leader of the Makiawisug (Little People of the Woodlands). The root of her name describes her very clearly. "Squa" means woman, blood, red, or of the earth. The root "anit" comes from "manit" or "Manitou", often spelled as "Mundu" in Mohegan-Pequot, which means Spirit. Therefore Granny Squannit's name means "SpiritWoman" and implies a connection to the earth and blood. . . . Quite literally, women are "the bleeders" through whose blood the tribe renews its life. Red is the color of the earth, hence the notion of "Mother Earth." . . . A woman Chief is known as a Sunq-Shquaaw, that is to day, she is the "Rock Woman" of the Tribe; since, the word "Sun[q] means rock in Mohegan Pequot."[6]

Besides the wonder of the contemporary powwow scene, the image of the noble savage—hostile still but righteously so—has impacted a number of Indians' idea of what it means to be Indian. Neither is it only leftist Americans who are enthralled by the idea of Indians-as-victims as proof that capitalist imperialism sucks. Although it is true that Native peoples have been victimized over the centuries, we are not victims, and because we did not cause the situation we find ourselves caught in, we cannot cure it, either. Resistance is futile, say the Borg on *Star Trek: The Next Generation*, and it may well be. It not only leads, as history has shown, to dead Indians, but it also divorces them from the very principles that vivify our ways to give them, and us, meaning.

The most recent case in point is the demand by some Indians that the exhibits at the newly opened National Museum of the American Indian be about the dreadful history of genocide (which has been fairly unsuccessful, I am happy to point out). This position requires that indigenous people from both North and South America take adversariness as their public position. *Don't be Indians*, it suggests, *don't use the most foundational parts of tradition as your path through life. Give it up: Be "Indian" as Anglo-Europeans define Indians: put on your buckskins, paint your face, don your feathers, and go to wars.* How can we be "braves" and "chiefs," otherwise?

Nevertheless, Indians were not particularly fond of conflict, as both traditional histories and ancient traditions show, nor are we defined by whether we look and act like Hollywood Indians (which hardly anyone does, or for that matter, ever did). To my mind, what defines Native thought is the advanced intelligence of it. Although there are hundreds of examples of this quality that range from instances of Native astronomy dating back to well before Europeans—or even the Vikings—came here to the way the various communities have adjusted Protestant American or Spanish Catholic norms to fit their original communal sense of identity, my favorite is Indian humor. One of the best-known Indian humorists, Vine Deloria Jr., passed away recently. The legacy he left will enlighten people for generations to come, I have no doubt. His work extended far beyond humor; he was, as one eulogist remarked, the foremost metaphysician and theologian in the United States in the twentieth century. The touchstone of his profound insights and discussions was his congenital ability to see the humor in the most terrible of circumstances.

In his hilarious and incisive *Custer Died for Your Sins: An Indian Manifesto* (1969), Deloria recounts a story about a missionary who is driving between Gallup and Albuquerque, "in the old days." Thinking he can perhaps make a conversion, the missionary pulls over and invites an Indian who is walking along the side of the highway to get in his car. After they have been driving east for a time, the missionary embarks on his program:

"Do you realize you are going to a place where sinners abound?"
　　The Indian nodded his assent.
　　"And," says the missionary, "the wicked dwell in the depths of their iniquities?"
　　Again, a nod.
　　"And sinful women who have lived a bad life go?"
　　A smile and then another nod.
　　"And no one who lives a good life goes there?" A possible conversion thought the missionary. And so he pulled out his punch line. "And do you know what we call that place?"
　　The Indian turns, looks the missionary in the eye and says, "Albuquerque."[7]

I learned how to use and to decode Indian humor from an early age. The entire Indian side of the family indulged in it, sometimes to my dismay, but mostly, particularly as I got old enough to follow at least some of the layers of irony in these anecdotes, to my delight. One of the major marks of high IQ and CQ (creativity quotient) is the ability to employ irony and ambiguity at several levels simultaneously. The more the levels, the greater the intelligence displayed. The only people I have met who equal Indians for this peerless ability are the English, and not only the comics but just about everyone, regardless of class.

Ook was probably the most intelligent of the family. My mother's youngest brother, he excelled at wordplay, an ability that many American Indians seem to have in spades. Although my whole family on the Laguna side was good at puns and intercultural jokes, Ook could top them all. When I was a teenager, we were talking about Darwin's theory of evolution and Ook said that Darwin proved that we were descended from spiders. At the time, I took in the information earnestly, thinking how that made sense because insects came before mammals, and so forth. It was not until years later that I realized the joke: According to Laguna epistemology, Grandmother Spider created everything, including the Lagunas, of course.

The kind of "cultural" and word play Ook enjoyed has been strongly echoed in my wanderings across Indian Country in both the United States and Canada. Indeed, I am taken aback when I meet a Native who does not laugh and joke around, so widespread is this highly developed wit. One measure of the great distance between Indian America and the rest of the nation is exactly that: an ability to find humor wherever one finds oneself, to make hilarity of the most invidious situations. A more life-affirming code of resistance and survival, I can scarcely imagine.

The Native American whom America knows and exports via the media is hardly the soul of wit. The Indian America loves is an earth-bound creature who is basically pious and close-mouthed or angry and vengeful, thus the lamenting Indian chief of the "don't be a litterbug" campaign or the righteously angry Indian student who demands the United States get out of North America (although perhaps the slogan is tongue-in-cheek). The only other stereotype of Native America seen as fit to honor is that of the Indian dead and gone but romantically tragic because of that fact.

It may come as a surprise to discover that the majority of Native people are practicing Christians; many are of various Protestant denominations, many are Roman Catholic. Once said, many Americans readily assume that Indian people are largely Christian because they were forced to accept Jesus as their savior by the conquering invaders. I imagined that to be the case for years but learned over time that conversion was quite a bit more traditionally Indian than modern European in its thrust. That is, the people—or I should say, the tribes and nations—converted because they saw benefit in taking on Christianity, but the benefit they saw was not "spiritual", as that rarefied process is understood among modern-day practitioners (although it was totally "spiritual" in the old, traditional sense).

They saw, quite rightly, that the Christians had access to a greater *powa* than what they could access at the time. Again, quite rightly, they wanted whatever *powa* they could use, so it seemed to them that mastering Christian methodologies would enable them to access this greater *powa*. In his 1936 novel *The Surrounded*, Chippewa-Cree Metís sociologist, anthropologist, and writer D'Arcy McNickle writes of how the Flathead, with whom he spent much of his life, became Christianized. Aware that tribes further east had been very lucky with their catch from the buffalo hunts, and that the Blackrobes (as the Jesuits were known) had been among them for some time, the Flathead Council determined that it, too, would invite the Blackrobes out to the mountains of western Montana, its homelands. The council sent two expeditions out to St. Louis, but the men did not return. A third expedition was successful, and the request was soon granted, or soon enough considering the speed of travel in the mid- to late-nineteenth century. The Flathead people took on Christianity, giving it their own stamp, as tribes did across North America.

John Smith writes of the Powhatan fascination with Western gadgets. Some men got hold of his compass and were very excited by it. "*Manitt, Manitou*," he said they kept repeating in great wonder. He attributed their response to "superstition"and recounted an anecdote in which he and his men dissuaded some other Indian men from a belief that was to the English another superstition of the same sort. However, seen from a traditional point of view, and given both the basic assumptions of those people at that time and the meaning of the word(s), they were saying "Divine," "Spirit" (or "Mystery"), the closest I can get here is "God, Godlike." Translating the sense of what they were saying as "magic!" or "sorcery!" might be closer, depending on the reader's point of view.

It seems to me that as long as we are accepting Euro-American practices in our lives, we might as well stick to the ones we are familiar with, those in which we have learned to keep alive the old ways while creating bridges to the new. One item absent from much political theory and practice is humor; another is the recognition of the profoundly nonmaterial character of life on planet Earth. In both regards, it bears a powerful kinship with Protestantism. Both concentrate on social organization, opposition to the status quo, and material acquisition. The two, "democratic capitalism" and Protestantism, are founded on the principle of exclusivity; that is, there is a pyramid of being, whether they are the owners or the saved, and from this peak all good things flow.

Although Native peoples were and are acquisitive, they characterized "stuff" as either unimportant or connected to the nonmaterial nature of the Earth around, below, and above. Even today, sharing via a variety of gifting methods, tribally practiced, is as widespread as ever. "Give-aways" as they are often called—we called them "Grab Days" at home—can be found even at powwows. Indeed, for Native people, gifting is a requirement, not as a matter of charity but as a manner of distributing wealth. It is not about peaks and trickles but about reciprocity, a sharing, equals to equals, of whatever affluence the community has acquired.

I see little point in privileging one Western point of view over another. Because both Marxism, the theoretical underpinning of leftist activism, and Protestant-cum-democratic capitalism, the underpinning of North American Euro-American society, are both European in origin, neither has much to do with tribal consciousness, traditional primary assumptions about the nature of reality, or the resulting social organization. As for resistance via conflict as methodology of restoring harmony and balance to the world, it does not compute. Lagunas (or those Lagunas who raised me) fervently believe that in no way can we garner harmony from conflict, although we can resolve conflict and enable any situation to return to its natural state (i.e., balance) via humor. As I spent most of my adult years learning about and visiting other kinds of Indians, I discovered that substituting humor for fisticuffs or "discipline" is a widespread method of maintaining social balance, which was and is essential to traditional ways of life.

As I see it, either we laugh a lot and keep on being NDN (Indian), or we become white men in feathers and ribbon shirts who prefer a big conflagration over the ancient ways of peace, harmony, balance, kinship, and integrity. Granted, the latter is by far the more difficult. However, it is also the way of the Elders since time immemorial.

I often dream that bunches of us, Indian and all other interested parties, converge on Washington and take our place before the Capitol building and the White House to mount a 24/7 laugh-in. At the very least, our health would improve; more, what makes Native America a unique community within the nation as a whole is our ability to see the ironic nature of the human condition and laugh. We could intersperse the hilarity with drumming, round-dance dancing, and a good "49" session. That's because 49s, which may also have come from Haskell experiences, are for laughing, courting, and generally having a good time.

The songs called 49s tell us that. "You said that you loved me sweetheart, but every time I call on you, you've always got another one; you know damn well that I love you, sweetheart. Way-ya hey hey ya. Way-ya he, he, ya," goes one. There are others. One I like has a line about going somewhere in "my one-eyed Ford." Native writers have taken their lead from the tradition of humor in social interactions, many writing poems, essays, and entire books in that vein. The one-eyed Ford is the subject of an early poem of Ojibwa-Chemahuevi poet Diane Burns. One of the funniest protests against either type of genocide, physical or cultural, that I have ever read is the short story "Zuma Chowt's Cave" by Chocktaw writer Opel Lee Popkes. "My relatives are smart; they married rich Indians. I married an illiterate Irishman who gave my oil rights away," jokes Popkes's mom when her daughter asked her why their branch of the family did not have any oil rights.[8]

Shoshone-Chippewa poet nila northSun's scathing ironies-cum-poems provide yet another model for how we have kept on keeping on over the centuries. Of course, the famed humorists Will Rogers and Vine Deloria Jr. exemplify the work of male Indian writers who retained their Indian identity while writing and speaking with tongue firmly in cheek. Readers may remember: Cherokee humorist and counselor to presidents Will Rogers is frequently quoted for joking: "I belong to no organized political party. I'm a Democrat!"

While I was working on this piece, I received an email from a former colleague from American Indian Studies at UCLA. The subject line read: "Taking Back the Country One Joke at a Time." That is what I mean: Synchronicity, or if you will, Tricksterism, a fundamental tribal basic principle. Even physics recognizes that there is always "the X factor," which must be taken into account in one's calculations.

Although the kind of humor I am talking about goes far beyond funny anecdotes, in the interests of encouraging a more tribal approach to life in Indian Country, I offer the following stories:

When White Man came, he said he wanted a piece of land about the size of a hide. Then he proceeded to slice the hide into thin, thin strips, making a long, long string. He made that the boundary between what he took as his land and what he said was ours (told me by a Cherokee friend).

"Why do you not put your red children on wheels, the better to move them around," pointedly asked one tribal leader of the president of the United States.

An Indian man and his dog were sitting on the sidewalk near downtown Pierre, South Dakota, when a white man with a straw hat came by. "Say, Chief," he said. "Is that a turd hound you've got there?"

"Why?" responded the Indian man. "Did he snap at you?"

My all-time favorite, though, uses a standard joke format, but with a twist:

Question: "How long is a Pueblo Grand Entry?"
Answer: "Three feet high and a mile long."

Finally, some bumper stickers I have known and loved:

- If You're Indian, You're In.
- Indian Affairs Are the Best.
- Custer Wore Arrow Shirts.
- Give Them an Inch and They'll Take 2,576,000 Square Miles.

And, remember:

- Of Course You Can Trust the Government. Ask Any Indian!

As they said at the Pueblo back in the old times when I was young, that long is my aunt's backbone.

NOTES

1. William Brandon, *The Last Americans: The Indian in American Culture* (New York: McGraw-Hill, 1973).

2. Luke E. Lassiter, *The Power of Kiowa Song: A Collaborative Ethnography*, October 4, 1998, on University of Arizona Press homepage, accessed November 17, 2005, at www.uapress.arizona.edu/extras/kiowa/kiowasng.htm.

3. "The Gourd Dance," Wyandotte Nation of Oklahoma Web site, posted November 1, 2005, accessed November 30, 2005 at www.wyandotte-nation.org/community/the_dances.html.

4. Rupert A. Ross, *Dancing with a Ghost: Exploring Indian Reality* (Toronto: Reed Books, 1992), pp. 8–40.

5. Marge Bruchac, "Reclaiming the Word 'Squaw' in the Name of the Ancestors," posted November 1999. Accessed on December 22, 2005, at www.nativeweb.org/pages/legal/squaw.html.

6. Melissa Jayne Fawcett [Tantaquidgeon], *The Lasting of the Mohegans, Part I: The Story of the Wolf People* (Uncasville, CT: Mohegan Tribe, 1995), p. 35.

7. Vine Deloria Jr., *Custer Died for Your Sins* (New York: Macmillan, 1969), p. 155.

8. Kenneth Rosen (ed.), *The Man to Send Rain Clouds: Contemporary Stories by American Indians* (New York: Vintage Books, 1975), p. 175.

CHAPTER 2

Decolonizing Native Women

~

Lee Maracle

National self-determination was advanced on the west coast of British Columbia as an alternative to the historic oppression that all Indigenous people have suffered in Canada by a group of young Native people before the close of the 1960s.

This was not the first movement to "decolonize." We were, however, unaware of the history of our struggle to decolonize. Our access to our own history had been aborted, not through choice, not accidentally, but deliberately, systematically, and cruelly. We had been, generation to generation, striving to hang on to the threads of our past through repeated struggles and losses for some 150 years on the west coast of BC, from which I herald, and for some 400 years on the eastern areas of the continent.

Some of us survived this struggle. We have survived not just the deliberate and systematic attempt to decimate our population, disperse us, and cut the threads of trade and commerce that existed prior to colonization, but we have also survived without access to knowledge, both Western and Indigenous.

I am ultimately concerned about the politics and governance of national self-determination. I am ultimately concerned about the political direction that the struggle of all our peoples to decolonize takes. Before I can begin to take up the banners that many Native men uphold as the ultimate goal—self-governance, an end to home rule by Canada and the United States—I need to retrace my own steps, the steps of my mother, my grandmother, my great-grandmother, right back to our original selves. I need to re-view their journey and reclaim the cultural base upon which we organized ourselves and our communities. I need to know how it came to pass that Native women are no longer valued, treasured, and protected inside our villages. I need to know how it came to pass that "women's issues" exist separately from men's. I need to know how our men came to decide what the standard of normal for women ought to be. I need to know how it came to be that our women are the most violated human beings, the least educated, the most overworked and underloved and unprotected human beings in the history of Turtle Island.

We all need to know who we were before and who we will be in the future. I have some very uncomfortable questions for the Native men who claim to lead our people. I want to know how many of them were selected based on their clear understanding of the past and their clear sense of direction into the future by people who understood their past when they chose them to chart the journey into the future. I need to know how many of the "voters" of elected band councils knew that their elders, long since dead, had objected to the electoral process being imposed upon us against the voices of the women who once held the power to stand chiefs up. I need to know how many of the voters selected the chiefs and councils that exist today based on open dis-cussion about the integrity, the spiritual cleanliness, the capacity to hear and respond appropriately to the women in the village, their capacity to protect the village, to ensure no harm came to the women and the children of the village. I need to know how many of our chiefs were selected based on their understanding of our original laws and not the laws of the outside world. How many were selected based on their commitment to rebuild the governing institutions of the past?

Native women have been asked to back-burner their issues as though the rematriation of our governing structures were somehow separate and secondary to nation building. We have, by and large, acqui-esced. We have stood on the barricades alongside men who violated our cousins, our sisters, and often ourselves and stood silent. We did so in the interest of national unity, in the interest of "the struggle," the "movement" for self-determination, as though we were not citizens, as though we were not really part of our own national governing systems.

We did so in the hope that some day, some day, someone would see us, recognize our greatness, our loyalty, and include us in the process. We did so without knowing that, to claim cultural integrity, national separateness, national identity, we would have to reclaim our knowledge of the past and take charge of the institutions that were originally our realm of governance.

Some of us were apprehensive about standing next to men who could back-burner violence against women and children, as though we were secondary issues and not central to the vision of future. Some of us became diehard feminists, Western style, to be ridiculed and ostracized by Native men. I respect those women. I believe they have been lied to, not just by Western colonialism but by their own leaders. I believe it is convenient for the current elected chiefs, and the colonial system that holds them up, to remain culturally blind to their real origins.

I understand from listening to men that they were lied to, that it is not "their fault," that they did not sit down and plot our violation. No one sitting in the living rooms of the villages arose and said, "Hey, I have an idea. Let's all be poor, get drunk, and beat and rape our women and children." No one did that. However, from the very moment that we all decided to rebuild our nations, from that very moment in 1968 on west coast of British Columbia, the restoration of all the power institutions within our nations should have been on the agenda, but they were not. From the very moment that political self-determination and economic development was on the agenda, the original governing structures of our past and the place of women should have been brought forward, but they were not.

I understand that men were lied to. I have been involved in the politics of self-determination and decolonization for almost thirty years. I know our men have been lied to. I have watched them uncover lie after lie, treachery after treachery, from a very male perspective.

I have watched them decipher the lies and the treachery in a way that bolsters male power and demeans our original governing systems.

I listened to an elder unravel the history of economic paralysis contrived by Canada to keep us poor. He named the "tricks" used by the Canadian legal system to ensure that each time we recovered from the deliberate impoverishment of Native people, we were sling shotted back into a state of poverty more desperate than before. At no time did this elder ever mention that the original economy was managed by women, the great sociological governesses of the past who held jurisdiction over the land, the wealth of families, or that it was the uprooting of this matriarchal system that opened the door to inequity, shame, and violence in our world.

I have listened to countless men speak of the matriarchy from which they come, who control the family wealth, control its internal distribution, and who, when they divorce their wives, retain the home, the business, and the wealth accumulated. I have heard men who come from a matriarchy say that this or that man "gave his home to his wife" when they were divorced. In a matriarchy, the home and the aggregate wealth of the family are not his to give.

I have listened to countless men oppose Western "human rights legislation for women" coming into our communities because it is a "political invasion" from the outside. I have not heard these same men stand up and tell our leadership, "Shame on you, for taking a post, dawning a chieftainship, that women have not sanctioned." I have not heard these men stand up and pose rematriation as the alternative to Western legal invasion.

In the vacuum of protection afforded by the restoration of matriarchy, I appreciate and respect the efforts of women to end the violence by insisting on the least we can achieve in the twenty-first century: women's rights and human rights protection. Make no mistake, however: I do not agree with the women who advocate "equal rights" for Native women under Western laws. Human rights legislation is the least we can expect. The present masks the consolidation and entrenchment of the subnormal for our women, just as they present the consolidation and entrenchment of the subnormal for Canadian women.

We must be protected. That is the bottom line. One way or another, Native women must end the violent condition accorded us. This acceptance at the least, however, ought not to define the goal or our normality. I am not in favor of throwing in the towel for the least we can expect.

I grew up under colonial conditions. I have a mature sensibility. Life has become simple for me. I want the most, the best, the fullest that life can present. Our cultures of the past created human beings who were self-reliant, self-disciplined, loving, and sharing, powerful beings. In our collectivity, we produced extraordinary individuals. In our spiritual maturity, we created humans who relied on their own spiritual discipline and vision, not an external supreme being or divine providence to guide us. We relied on public accountability and our personal social conscience to police ourselves, not an armed body of goons to occupy our villages and force us to behave.

Our systems of organization were cognizant of the smallness of humanity in the general web of life, as well as our own personal spiritual significance in the governance and realization of life. Women had dominion over the social relations of the nation and the education of our children, not as executors who merely followed some curriculum estranged from the life and environment in which we arose but as those who developed the process of education of the children, the curriculum presented to them, and who determined who should execute the actual teaching of the children. We had command of the economy of our nations, the pedagogy of our young, and the governance of the relationships among the citizens of our nations.

Western society is an alienated society. Its individuals have come to accept the estrangement of spiritual belief, emotional wellness, physical existence, knowledge, and intellectual development from the central fire from which they arise. Walk around the neighborhood of any white community and ask the individuals within the homes exactly what aspect of their society they can say they influence or manage. None. Not even the graduates of their cultural institutions manage the education process. Everything is preset in a mold that began shaping before the Greco-Roman cultural ascendance some 2,000 years ago. Everything that exists in their world today is born of that mold.

We have inherited the castings from the mold, bits and pieces, the leftovers, the guidelines with very little of the cultural benefits. This inheritance is a personal and social, political and economic, cultural and spiritual, gender- and race-based inequity. No single piece of the inequity we inherited is disconnected from the general nature of Canadian class- and gender-based inequity. However, in a pyramid society, the lower layers all seem to struggle to gain some of the benefits of the layer just above them. White women want the advantages accorded to white men, Native men want the advantages accorded white men, Native women want the advantages accorded to white women, and so forth. The picture we all have of white men is distorted to begin with.

We tend to view them as having some sort of opportunity to alter the political, social, and economic relations that govern them. We tend to view them as possessing the permission fundamentally to alter the conditions from which they arise. Nothing could be further from the truth.

White men struggle from a place of power. This power is rooted not in their own social reality but in the power we, as those on the bottom, vest in them. It is a spiritual power of belief that we, as Native men, Native women, and white women, accord them. They struggle from a place of "cultural respectability and acceptance" accorded to them by one another and by those on the lower levels of society.

Reality is always false. This belief, acceptance, and respectability are rooted in the absence of lateral respect among ourselves. Even those who object to our disbelief in ourselves accuse "white male power" as the culprit who corroded this disbelief. We are all like a group of sibling children, hollering "Unfair!" to one another, while the authors of the unfairness get off scot-free.

As Native women, we look at the conditions we are immersed in and view "human rights legislation" as fair. This is a cheap comparison to what existed prior to colonization. It is today a dangerous request; we may get what we pray for. Twenty percent of white women live below the poverty line, and 20 percent live above it, which means that 60 percent live at the line. Those 60 percent living at the line belong to double-income households. This means that, if those men and women were to divorce, all of them would fall below the poverty line. It also means that, if one half of the couples in this 60 percent fall out of work, they would both fall below the line.

When white people lose their jobs, they lose their homes. Culturally, they do not have relatives who will take them in. There is an inherent insecurity in being Canadian and white. In most of our communities, it is still assumed that when a woman divorces her husband, she keeps the home and the children, unless she chooses not to raise her children. Furthermore, it is also assumed in many communities that the children have choices, too.

The more Canadian legal sensibility invades our communities, the greater the corrosion of the rights of children and women. Whether a woman gains custody of her children is based on her financial ability to provide for them. Whether she keeps the home is often dependent upon how much she paid for it, the credibility of her lawyer, and the effort her lawyer is willing to invest in her future. The investment of homemaking has no dollar value. Native women are the most chronically underemployed and unemployed people in Canada. No judge would rule in their favor.

Almost half of Native women in Canada do not legally marry, nor do they divorce, through the courts. Of those couples who have legally married, many of the men plead "no contest." Thus, we women generally gain custody of our children, and our homes are left to us. The loss of the husband's income is generally nominal, as most Native men are not high wage earners. What we lose is valuable assistance in the rearing of the children, if the man was a decent father, or the violence, if he was not. At home, in our communities, we have access to family support, which tends to minimalize the loss.

The "good mother" comparative scenario that invades many white women's future does not invade our right to our children or our homes. We currently have more choices than do white women. What we do not have is financial security. Guess what, ladies: Neither do most Native men.

Those who are calling for a human rights invasion of our world generally live outside our communities, are educated, and thus have greater opportunity for employment than do most Native people, male or female. Educated Native women do not have equal access to jobs or power in the hierarchy erected by Canada, funded by Canada, in our world. The feminist response to inequity does not stand to enhance their "place" in our world.

Reality is always false. The current "band" government structures, the tribal government structures, the community agencies, and the nongovernmental organizational structures from which Western European power can be acquired, exist at the goodwill and financial capability of Canada to continue to fund those structures. This financial capability is imploding, and cutbacks to Indigenous people is, and always has been, Canada's first response. The capacity for the economic recovery of Canada hinges on global economics, not goodwill. This makes the feminist response power-suicide for most Native women.

I respect the response. It is rooted in a clear perception of our current reality. However, I believe our elders when they said, "Reality is always false." I was very young and inexperienced when I asked my grandfather why we continued to promote kindness, gentleness toward white people, when the truth is, they can apathetically watch us die, or promote our death. This is our reality, not their truth. The truth is that it is inhuman apathetically to watch a people die, or promote their demise. The truth is, everyone is born perfect. Imperfections and poison fed to them resulted in this reality. We need to continue to feed them a different meal, until they change, and that will alter our reality. The truth will remain the same.

Reality is transitory and in flux. At the time I asked this, I was still burning with rage at the memory of white youth terrorizing our reserves and the many attempted rapes white men wrought on my person. Today, our children and particularly our daughters face the same violence and rape, but the faces have changed. Today, it is our own men who perpetrate this violence in our world. The belief from the outside world about our value has invaded us, but it is not the truth.

Racism and sexism are cultural beliefs that invade all aspects of our perception of ourselves. They invade our perception of cultural integrity from the past. They invade our research of the past; they invade our perception of economic development, political decision making, national legislation, governance, education, and social development. They create a reality for Native men and women. They invade our personal perception of one another as man and woman. They invade our homes.

The reality for men is loss of power in their relationship with Canada. The reality for women is loss of power over the social relations inside our families and the economics of our internal world. What holds these realities in place are our beliefs about ourselves and transference of those beliefs to one another.

Suppose men did not believe in the loss of power in their relationship to Canada. Suppose, for example, they went hunting when it was time to hunt, regardless of the laws Canada attempted to impose upon them. Suppose they decided simply to down logs in the territory surrounding their villages and build homes, despite their lack of access to the logs in our original territories and the "standards" for homes imposed by Canada. Suppose they insisted that Canada prove its ownership of the logs, fish, animals, and so forth in our original territories. Suppose every Native man in Canada called upon the government to provide the piece of paper transferring title from ourselves to them, proving they owned it all in the first place.

Canada cannot prove ownership or jurisdiction over the original homelands of the vast majority of Indigenous people. The best it can prove is surrender of access due military defeat. Current Canadian law contravenes Canada's right to invade another nation and usurp its lands. Should Native men decide to do these things, the need for expensive constitutional lawyers, civil suits, and consultants would end.

Suppose women decided tomorrow that there would be zero tolerance for violence within our homes. Suppose we all stopped neglecting our children, punishing them for our condition, and refused to maintain homes with violent men living within their walls. Suppose we all joined together and informed men that they would be removed from our homes if they chose to be violent. Suppose we decided to remove men rather than agreeing to give up our homes and build shelters for abused women and children. We would be in violation of Canadian human rights. Suppose we said, our laws clearly state that the home, the gardens, the river's fish, the village itself, is the dominion of women, and we as women are assuming our inherent aboriginal right to exercise the dominion of our homes and villages.

Should women do this, the need for Canadian human rights legislation and the organizations that advocate such rights would end. This action would contravene a central belief we have dragged home: that their law, their world, is superior to our own. There is a journey to this belief, and there is a journey to its undoing. It is not self-governance to take up another nation's legal system and entrench it in our nations. There is no cultural integrity in guiding our actions based on external beliefs. There is no spirituality, which is rooted in a condition created by external spiritual beliefs. Zero tolerance for violence is not a sufficient goal. The restoration of our original institutions of power, management, authority, choice, permission, and jurisdiction is what nationhood is all about.

Culturally, Native societies were either colineal or matrilineal. There were clear delineations of jurisdiction and authority between men and women, between adults and children, between elders and the young, between families, clans, and nations. These lines of authority have been muddied by our current and historical journey to our reality.

Prior to the arrival of the British and French on the shores of Turtle Island, First Nations peoples occupied distinct territories. Together, these nations had access to unlimited wealth. This access, however, was tempered and restricted by spiritual belief systems, which acknowledged the "place" of every living creature, including the Earth as a living entity. The temperance and restriction were held up by common ascription to the belief in them throughout Turtle Island. All of our systems of governance, our oracy, our codes of conduct, our ceremonies, and our language held up these beliefs.

We maintained ourselves in bioregionally specific areas as independent societies. Turtle Island supported a number of Nations whose culture varied widely from one another. Despite differences in language, customs, and laws, First Nations societies ascribed to the belief in a spirit-to-spirit relationship between themselves and all members of creation. Elaborate systems of government promoted peace within the nation, among themselves, and with other Nations, as well as between themselves and the Earth.

Peace was not seen as a given. Our stories indicate that opportunism is essential to our survival as humans. In the *Stoh:loh* story, this opportunism is seen as unconscious, unintentionally taking advantage of the power inherent in being a spirit. Flora, Fauna, Humans—all begin as thought or hidden being, emotion, spirit, mind. Eventually, things came to such a pass that Raven and Eagle called the spirit world to the first "great spiritual gathering." A conscious decision to take on physical being was made. From this came creation. Stone alone was innocent in all of this, so it alone does not have to go through the life, death process; it just is. This story is told without judgment. The lesson I draw is that we as humans were creating the most havoc and, therefore, were seen as the most opportunistic, and hence we hold a greater responsibility to come to grips with consequences.

Over time, we were given tools by our great thinkers, who learned from life, transforming what we learned into "Raven stories of transformation and growth," recited during the long winter months of leisure. This opportunism is seen as neutral, neither positive nor negative. It is a constant, not a variable. What is variable is our capacity for being conscious. Humans can consciously temper this inherent opportunism in a positive or negative direction. This direction of positive and negative capacity is acknowledged without judgment or condemnation in our origin story. However, later on, in our first war story, the story of the war between the bird and animal kingdom, the personal opportunism of the bat met with dire consequences. This first war was inspired by hardship, which led to violence and opportunistic lifestyles of murder, infanticide, and cannibalism. The opportunism of the whole was rooted in survival of the few. Bat's opportunism, however, took shape during the process of resolution. There is recognition that opportunism has no place in the process of resolution.

Wrapped around the recognition of this capacity is an understanding of the conditions under which the optimum capacity for human positive expression and direction are delineated. Survival is a problem for all living beings. The choice is to take advantage of the problem, push up our best thinking collectively to solve it, or to stay stuck in the problem, take advantage of the collective thinking to ensure we are on the winning side. This war is seen pragmatically as an obstacle to the most positive human expression of direction.

We are not against war under any and all circumstances. War is the inability of humans to come to a creative, collective resolution. War is an expression of the underdevelopment of human beings. War is seen as defensive, not aggressive, for the purpose of conquest. It is seen as an obstacle to the positive internal development of the Nations who engage in it. Hence, after engagement in war, the men who had killed were stood at the edge of the forest and cleaned off before reentering the village. Internal peace was primary. Wars occurred over jurisdiction, sometimes trade, and during hardship, when survival was threatened, and one Nation invaded the territory of another to ensure its own survival. We respect other Nations who are prepared to go to war to ensure the survival of their people. We respected World War II, but not the first of 1914, World War I.

Processes for demarcating territorial survival areas were developed by men. The jurisdiction of each nation was carefully negotiated between Nations, and structures existed for the resolution of conflicts between families, villages, and nations. We developed the language of diplomacy carefully, thoughtfully, with diligence and discipline. There are strict guidelines governing how we approach someone who has invaded our territory. If you have hard truths to offer up to someone, make sure the voice is soft, the language beautiful, and protect the dignity of the other. When the storm clears, make sure you all see sunshine.

We lost this voice, this language, so now we employ the Bambi rule of, "If you can't say anything nice, don't say anything at all." All hell can break loose, and we will lock our throats, tighten our chest, cross our arms, shake our legs, and bite our tongues to avoid saying anything at all. It does not occur to anyone that, maybe, we ought to reclaim the language of peace, exploration, and resolution. The laws that governed First Nations were recognized and embraced as the basis for mature decision making. They were rooted in the social praxis of each nation, which carefully structured the lives of its children, the expectations of those children to embark upon a journey that would result in adult being. The culture required that each child become a deep-thinking child with a consciousness that was fair, sharing, just, and caring. Oracy—stories of behavior and consequence—was the major disciplinary force exerted upon children.

The optimum health of each and every human soul was sought, extended, and guaranteed by law. We believed that "illness" led to misbehavior, poor diet; led to weakness of resolve. A weak body houses a weak mind, and a weak mind creates emotional disturbance. There was a direct link between poor health and misbehavior. The promise of the spirit-to-spirit relationship with our mother, the Earth, and the waters is that the plants, animals, and all life are here to support us in achieving the good life. All that is required of us is to acknowledge those beings who surrender their lives to us and to obey the laws we inherited from that which set all life into motion, the great mystery.

Access to food, clothing, and shelter were absolute. Rather than deny children food for ill-disciplined behavior, children who were ill-disciplined were viewed as inadequately fed. Herbal teas were administered to restore the good health they were entitled to. Physical prowess, agility, and strength were seen not as matters of individual idolatry or competition but as the necessary condition for the emotional, mental, spiritual well-being of every single individual.

The Earth was seen as a living entity, not as an object of conquest and exploitation. The rhythms of the Earth, its natural capacity for self-rejuvenation, were recognized and expected. We did not live all year 'roundin the same place, if during one season the tide rose, and during another, it fell. Likewise we did not live by rivers that flooded in the winter, during its flood season. We studied animal and plant behavior and aligned ourselves to it. We ate seasonally, in accordance with the rhythms of the Earth, careful to preserve what was not available to us all year-round in a way that was the least intrusive possible upon the natural rhythms of the Earth. Culturally, the Earth itself was the only being we were required to accommodate.

Our beliefs and the lifestyle that arose from those beliefs, required us to utilize every part of the plant and animal life we killed in our self-support.

The material culture which arose was largely biodegradable. That which was not biodegradable was handed down, human to human. Waste was returned to the Earth, not dumped in huge landfill sites. The laws governing production precluded the invention of items that would disrupt the rhythm of the Earth. Our creativity was structured within very narrow guidelines of respect, consideration, sharing, and caring. Our spiritual belief system formed the basis of our logic. No value, no law, no behavior existed outside the logic of our spiritual beliefs.

The beauty of our architecture on the west coast is that we took mature trees, turned them into houses; beautiful story poles adorned them; all our tools, clothing, utensils were contrived from these mature trees. The cutting down of these mature trees led to further plant and life development and made space for those younger trees to become mature. The house was made beautiful within the context of nonintrusive survival. Taste, aesthetics, was disciplined by making the most of the least. We had useless baubles, just like any other culture. There is nothing useful about a carved set of flutes, hair combs, spoons, feast bowls; once you have one, the need ends. However, once the house is built, there is a lot of leftover wood. The leftover wood became ornaments of art.

It was inconceivable for us to create art out of new materials. It was inconceivable that we could invent electricity because the damming of rivers ran counter to our spiritual belief that the river itself was alive, had a spirit, and hence, a perfect right to be. It was inconceivable that we could take it upon ourselves to dam a river because the flooding was a nuisance. This meant we had to move our homes further upland from its swelling banks—the river was alive; it had a right to be. Furthermore, many of the agrarian peoples, the Iroquois, Ojibway, and so forth, noted over time that flooding was ultimately beneficial to their corn-beans-squash-growing cultures. The river and its particular behavior was there to help them

The cultural practice of house building and location accommodated the river's behavior. Hence, the longhouses were in the center; the corn fields surrounded the longhouse, and the river edged the fields. Our entire medical practice centered on the specific nature of plant-animal support and was governed, not by symptoms of illness that appeared in the decrepit body, but rather by those symptoms that appeared before the body became decrepit. The slightest change in character was first fed; restlessness, impatience, change in breath, voice, and behavior: All were regarded as signs of illness.

There are behavioral changes in a baby before the baby's body exhibits illness. A crying baby is a hungry baby. Thus, special attention is paid to the food its mother receives while nursing. Women are attended to with a myriad of teas that prevent the development of premenstrual syndrome, the curse of women in the twentieth century. The development of young boys into manhood is attended to with a higher consumption of meat, berries, and greens than that of the men who have already achieved manhood. Young girls are administered hormone-regulating teas to support them in their change to womanhood, and so forth. There are behavioral changes in a human being before illness disrupts the natural processes of the body and results in decrepitness. An angry person is viewed as a hungry person, so teas are administered to resolve the hunger.

The Earth is not seen as a stupid, insensitive lump floating numbly throughout space to be conquered, pillaged, and plundered at will, but rather as an intelligent being with its own journey, its own way of resolving illness within itself. We see it as a human responsibility to become familiar with the patterned behavior of the Earth, ally ourselves with these patterns, and augment our life within the context of Earth's patterns or suffer the consequences.

The structure of authority was an extension of these belief systems. We recognized the balance between male and female, between plant and climate, between earth and water; we lived according to this balance. Jurisdiction between men and women was parceled out in accordance with the balance we saw in the natural world. Men had jurisdiction over the external world and the lands surrounding the villages. Women had jurisdiction over the harvesting of food. It was incumbent upon women to acquire the knowledge of this food, the amount required; planning the preservation, distribution, and consumption of the food fell within their direct authority. Permission to choose what one ate at any given moment did not exist. Consultation with men took place around the location of wild foods and the protection required during the harvest. The ceremonies governing the preharvesting generally fell within the realms of those who had direct jurisdiction over the lands from which the food was harvested.

It is a direct invasion of the authority of women over the general health and well-being of our communities to eat according to taste. A body that is not well-nourished is an anxious body; a body that is decrepit is not a body that can make decisions well; a body that is anxious makes anxiety-ridden decisions that are most often self- and mutually destructive. A body that eats for taste is not a sane, rational, or strong body.

Spiritual logic and practice governed our entire lives. We have no ceremony for passing from healthful eating to acquiring the right to eat for taste. We have no ceremony for women who wish to abdicate their authority over food preparation, distribution, or consumption. We have no stories extolling the virtues of sugar consumption, drug consumption, alcohol consumption. We have no ceremony for extolling the virtues of male domination of female authority over food and home. We have no ceremony for extolling the virtues of entitling our children to eat as they please.

The loss of this authority is directly connected to the loss of male jurisdiction over our national territory, their historic loss of authority to protect it, and the loss of our mothers' right to raise us. Our knowledge was passed on by word of mouth. It was during the course of our daily interaction that we taught our children. Through their daily lives, through the hearing of stories through participation in ceremonies, our children acquired the knowledge base necessary to wield the authority they were to acquire later on in life.

This process of proactive learning continued long after adulthood. The connection between well-behavior and wellness remained unbroken until residential school, compulsory education, and the outlawing of our cultural practices destroyed the family, clan, and political power structures necessary to pass on this knowledge. The loss of land base from which to access the foods was contingent. So thorough has the erosion of female authority been that few women today can make decisions within their homes free of consulting the smallest child without negative repercussions. So thorough has the erosion of male authority been that few men can decide to go out to secure food for their family without consulting some outside source without negative consequences. If women had their original authority over the internal social relations, including food preparation, consumption, and distribution, and the original knowledge base to wield this authority, men would have to find their own way back to reclaiming their authority in the external world. Human beings cannot live without authority, permission, choice, and jurisdiction. The rate of death among us, directly related to our social condition and the absence of the above in our daily lives, attests to the truth of this.

White men appropriated the cultural knowledge of women in the early days of colonialism. It was not extinguished among us until compulsory education in industrial training schools limited our knowledge base some hundred years after white men had written down much of our original medical knowledge. For almost one hundred years, we were sent to institutions that taught very few academic subjects and no medicine whatsoever. In fact, practicing medicine without a license is outlawed to this day. Jurisdiction over the quality of our common life, the authority to determine the optimum well-being of our common life, the permission to define internal wellness and to outline the social conditions, the framework within which choice is made, was our singular most powerful loss as women. In fact, many working women find that they have more authority outside the home on the job than they do inside the home.

I respect women who have taken up the Canadian feminist response, unlike those who dismiss them because they are "influenced from outside our world." I believe their feminism is in response to the internal male invasion of our areas of jurisdiction. Unlike those who condemn them for operating outside our culture, I understand that they are operating from within the current conditions. I also understand that those men who ascribe to the matriarchal nature of their original cultures and who decry Western feminism among us have not been proactive about the restoration of female governing institutions nor do they opt for full female power inside the home. The dismissal of these women silences the whole.

No one wants to explore our past jurisdiction if we are going to meet with negative results. What has happened is a strange commingling of men and women around original male power, knowledge, and authority. Men know a great deal about diplomacy, negotiations, politics, and war. Without female knowledge of conduct, health, wellness, and peace, they drag their bundle of knowledge into realms that are internal. To be heard, acknowledged, and respected, women must pick up the same bundle and engage in the same process of enmification of other men. Camps are established, factions hothoused, and the losses we incur are our own.

Men are not responsible for handing us our bundle of knowledge. However, the permission to do so must exist outside ourselves before we dare risk exercising this choice. When we speak from our own knowledge base, someone must be there to hear us, acknowledge the truth of our words, pick up the trail presented, and respond appropriately. We must gather ourselves together as women; reclaim our sociological knowledge, our medical knowledge, our right to determine the health standards of our nations and exercise our authority; acknowledge one another, challenge men to make real their commitment to the matriarchal and colineal societies of the past. The feminist response is equality outside the home. That sounds sensible to those who have never in their history exercised authority and jurisdiction over the internal social relations and economic distribution of wealth inside their communities. It sounds sensible if they believe that men have authority outside the home worth sharing. I just don't believe the trade-off works for us.

I believe traditional people have been reclaiming culture within the narrow band of male preponderance over us, not in accordance with their own jurisdiction over our national relations with the external world and their jurisdiction over our entire national territory. While speaking of "government-to-government relations," little attempt has been made to examine our original governing structures, and no thought has been given to the power and jurisdiction of women and the balance between them before going to the table with the Canadian government. Those doing the negotiating were "elected" in a blind contest, in which no discussion about the nature of chieftainship, the responsibilities embraced by it, the direction of the nations, the strategy for achieving the vision of the nation, or the breadth and extent of authority inherent in the chieftainship occurred. No discussion existed on whether the individuals in the running had the necessary skills, integrity, or capability to effect nationhood in the long run.

White societies' elections were described by the Rhinoceros Party as the "joy of fools," way back in the mid-1980s. I have participated in but two elections throughout my forty-six-year-old life. I did so because both candidates agreed to be stood up before their electorate and asked some extremely personal questions about the strength of their convictions and their personal integrity. Both candidates were elected. Despite the fact that they were consistently a minority, they maintained their integrity. If they had not, I would have had no problem organizing their voters and campaigners to challenge them—personally. That was back in 1973, when we were new to this election business. Up until that point, only 10 percent of our populations participated in their own internal elections. It is interesting to note that there is a general reluctance to revive the practice of open discussions about integrity and personal conviction.

We have since taken up the no-gossip standard of the external world so fiercely that we have no permission to discuss the integrity of those who are making national decisions for us. It is regarded as muckraking to mention that the Grand Chief of the Assembly of First Nations (AFN) walked out of his home, ostensibly to get a pack of cigarettes, never to return. The wife he left sued him for past support upon his election. I do not know the state of his marriage when he did this. I have no idea what his wife was like, but I know that nonsupport of children victimizes the innocent in that relationship. It is none of my business what he does personally, but I am curious to know what the effect that behavior will have on his national decision making around women and children and the obligations of fathers to support those children in the future. As a woman who feels very responsible for the future of our children, I want to know how he views his own actions of the past. I want to know whether he can make clear decisions re-garding the future of Native children. I want to know whether he has acquired a depth of commitment to children beyond his past behavior.

One of our British Columbia provincial leaders beat his common-law wife so badly, she had to be hospitalized for three weeks. He escaped charges because she simply divorced him without charging him. Some women called for his resignation. His colleagues affirmed his position. The discussion centered on the consequences for him. It would have been politically ruinous to force him to resign. The discussion on his political record centered on his commitment to Indian self-government and land claims. No discussion took place on the absence of his commitment to the end of violence against women in our world.

Previously, women conducted the selection of our leaders, and their behavior in the village, their forthrightness, their integrity, was a pri-mary subject of the discussion that took place. We chose the cleanest men to guide our affairs. We chose the men with the greatest integrity, the strongest, the most forthright and upright men, to handle our af-fairs without regard to their political career goals. The current election system of Europeans is a blind date that often goes sour. Date rape is the worst-case result of a blind date gone sour. According to a study done by the women of the Northwest Territories, fully 90 percent of women and children experience sexual assault. This means for us as women that abuse begins in childhood and does not end.

Men have limited dominion over village life, which they never had before. Their limited dominion is defined by the external world, which cancels out any notions of jurisdiction. They have been reduced to authorities over villages whose jurisdiction falls under Canada and its legal system. The only place they have any authority at all is in our homes, and it is a coercive authority based on negative repercussions for us women should we opt to exercise our traditional authority over the home and the social-political relations inside it.

Women are held hostage inside the home by the negative repercus-sions. Outside the home, we enjoy the same limited dominion as men. The roles have been somewhat reversed. It seems as though the only way women can establish healthy, happy futures for their children is to drive men out of the home. Almost half the Native women in my home area have done just that. This does not re-create a terribly bright future for our sons or our daughters, however. Many women have taken up struggling with male sexist attitudes, which seems to create a war zone between the sexes, constant conflict, and incessant bickering. There is a man I know who finds himself witty and clever and who has his own running joke about whether the toilet seat should be left up or down. He maintains that it is inconsiderate of women to leave it down, rather than return it to its upright position. He finds it amusing that he and the women in his house continually debate this question. I find it amusing myself that a man whose ancestors held dominion over five million acres of New York state, participated in the management of an entire Confederacy of Six Nations, influenced the peace and well-being between this Confederacy and the several dozen nations surrounding it, including the United States and Canada, would sell himself so short as to quibble over a toilet seat. I do not find it amusing that he has so little respect for the authority of the women in his house to govern a thing so small as a toilet seat.

No woman would divorce over something as small as a toilet seat. Dominion over the house, however, is exacted over the small, the mundane, the uneventful little things that make life in the outer world bearable, powerful, and meaningful in the long run. No one would divorce over such a thing as jurisdiction over what food is purchased, consumed, and how it is distributed within the family. In the outside world this would be considered laughable: I divorced him because he insisted on feeding my children Kool-Aid, or he demanded to eat white bread instead of white corn.

No one divorces over what paintings are purchased, hung on the wall, what appliances, what or games are purchased, what toys the children receive, whether or not summer vacation is spent berry picking or going to Disneyland. These things may be a constant source of argument and debate, civil and uncivil, but no one divorces over them. No one divorces over a man's refusal to eat certain foods because they do not taste good. No one divorces over a man's refusal to take vitamin supplements because he is cranky, and we know vitamins would solve it. We will argue, cajole, persuade, but we will not divorce him for it.

These things are small things, too small to disrupt the entire family over. These small things, however, are largely responsible for the disruption of family in general. Bad food leads to bad behavior. Bad food leads to poor health and decrepitude and, finally, death. As women, we once had jurisdiction over life. We were the governesses of the quality of life and the social relations within the family. We knew this was hinged to adequate food. We knew what foods created the best possible human beings. We had the authority in our homes free of coercion. The women owned the house and all that was in it, except for the man's tools. The man had the right to eat and was required to express appreciation for the food provided. Men participated with women in ensuring that there was adequate food. They were directed by women as to what that food was and how much was required.

I have no idea what sort of negotiations with other nations were required for men to hop on a large canoe and go out and secure a few hundred ocean salmon, some seals, oolichans, or whales. I do know that several different nations inhabited the west coast, that all of those nations fished the same areas, that those areas were managed by men at the behest of women who determined the amount required. White historians maintain that the men of the west coast aboriginal nations fought over fishing grounds, whaling territories, and so forth. I have no comment on whether that is true. I do know that our men must have solved these problems because prior to colonization, we did not experience hunger. Perhaps they did war over fishing grounds; that may be the reason polygamy existed on the west coast. War, generally, reduces the male rather than the female population. Polygamy is the general human response to an inadequate male population.

What I do know is that the lives of the women and children were valued by men. They did what they needed to do to secure our future. They risked their lives at sea, in the interest of an adequate food supply for those women and children. If the condition of chronic war is true, they risked national peace in the interest of the future of women and children. They did so at the behest of the women inside their villages. If, as some of our elders maintain, war was not common but, rather, that diplomacy between men existed, it changes nothing for us as women.

Jurisdiction over food, its procurement, consumption, distribution, and the concomitant health and well-being was determined by women. Whatever route those men took was entirely up to them. Once the women selected the clan heads, the chiefs, the speakers, and so forth, their involvement in the process of securing peaceful relations between villages and between the nations became a consultative one solely at the discretion of those leaders. The women informed their leaders of the food requirements of the village, and the men set out, organized themselves, and through either war or diplomacy, they met those requirements.

Because women did not have authority over the diplomatic relationships between nations, we ensured that we raised thinking men, sensitive men, clear-headed men, men who could wield diplomacy, men who were mature enough to persuade, cajole, and convince others that sharing was the best policy. That our men were capable of sharing with the citizens of foreign nations is clear from the original contact between white men and Native men. Initial contact was sometimes friendly, sometimes not, depending on the behavior of the white men. When we were met with adversity, contact was not friendly.

Charlie Jones, a Nuuchalnuuth elder, recounts his story. First contact was not friendly, war ensued, and most of the white men were killed, their heads shrunk and added to the belts of those who participated in the war. Second contact, the intruders said they had a holy man aboard—a man of peace. Armed only with gifts, they allowed this man ashore. The holy man set smallpox blankets under each big house, some hundred in all; smallpox devastated the village. Most died. Incapacitated, they were unable henceforth to resist invasion. Charlie summed up his life experience by saying, "We should have killed them all."

CHAPTER 3

Weeping for the Lost Matriarchy

~

Kay Givens McGowan

Before the Europeans, Southeastern Natives lived in matriarchal cultures, but today, it is painful for us to examine our old societies. Too often, modern Native women are "strong" only in comparison to their disempowered brothers. What has been lost is everything. If, however, there is any hope of restoring Native society, of saving our children, our brothers—ourselves—knowing how we once lived may give us some guidance.

The great Native American civilizations of the Southeast of the present-day United States—importantly including the Cherokee, Choctaw, Chickasaw, Muscogee, and Seminole—were matriarchal societies. In them, women, as equals of the men, had power and influence. All of this changed with the coming of the Europeans, who assumed that Native people lived as Europeans did, in patriarchal systems, in which elite men defined the "appropriate way" for women to behave. They failed to understand the equality of the sexes in Native American societies, where women enjoyed high economic, social, and political status.

Economically, the Southeastern nations were agricultural people. Women farmed and controlled the crops that their work produced, so they were often the traders. This set of responsibilities was confusing to and frequently misunderstood by the early Europeans with whom they traded. In their imposed patriarchy, European men just assumed Native societies were like the male-dominated societies of Europe, in which the economy rested entirely in male hands.

Because they were farmers, however, Native women performed the work that low-status men did in Europe, where the farm work was done by serfs who never controlled the land and who were not entitled to its bounty. Each year, the crops belonged to their landlords. By contrast, Native women viewed the Earth as their Mother, who gave life to the plants, just as they, the women, gave life to their children. Instead of being drudges in a hierarchical and exploitative situation, as serfs were in Europe, Southeastern women considered the planting and harvesting of food rewarding, for the bounty realized was theirs to dispose of as they saw fit. In the matriarchal societies of the Southeast, women worked cooperatively for the good of everyone.

Rights to farmlands and their produce did not end the economic powers of Southeastern women. Women had ownership rights. For instance, they owned the houses, the crops, and the lineages. As eighteenth-century naturalist William Bartram observed in 1791 after visiting the Muskogees ("Creeks") and the Cherokees, "Marriage gives no right to the husband over the property of his wife."[1] That Native women could own property was a shock to the Europeans, who believed that men had the sole right to own and control all property. Even their women and children were considered their property.

When English and French traders sought skins, furs, corn, and other products, they had to trade with women, engendering apprehension and uncertainty in the Europeans. As a result, they often refused to trade with the women, but it was not until the mid-1700s that the heel of British oppression came to rest firmly on the backs of Native women. Being the greatest power in the "colonies" by 1763, the British dominated and controlled the territories, laying down the law not just on economic issues but also on social and political issues.

Socially, contrary to European patrilineal expectations, Southeastern societies traced their ancestry through the women. Children were born into the clan of their mother, where they remained their entire lives. This descent pattern is called matrilineal and was common in many more Native American societies than just the Southeastern. Across Turtle Island (North America), generations of mothers, daughters, and granddaughters formed large social units that made up the clans, as well as individual lineages.

The power of matrilineage was reinforced by our matrilocal residence patterns. When a couple married, they lived with, or very near, the woman's family. Often, a young bride, her mother, her sisters, and their families all lived with the bride's maternal grandmother. Matrilineage combined with a matrilocal residence pattern formed the basic family structure of Southeastern societies.

The descent pattern, along with the residence patterns, gave power to the women of the nation. When a woman married, she worked and bore children for her own lineage, not her husband's. Her role as mother was more important than her role as wife. Men might come and go, but children remained a woman's children for life.

If a woman tired of her man, she could take her children and leave— or rather, *he* could leave. In the case of a divorce, the husband returned to the clan house of his mother. The life of his children remained unchanged in the home of their mother, except that their father no longer lived there. Consequently, in divorce, the matrilocal residence pattern was nondisruptive to children, who were the most important consideration in Indian societies.

The women of the Southeastern nations had much more freedom than European women living in their nuclear families because all of the women of the Native family shared in the tasks of child care and childrearing. From the perspective of the children, they had unconditional love from aunts and grandmothers, as well as from their biological mothers. They felt the security of a large extended family, which meant that there were a significant number of people they could count on the rest of their lives for help, love, acceptance, and security.

Southeastern women also had sexual freedom, unlike women in Europe. The Europeans had two notions about women. Either they were "decent," meaning chaste until marriage, or they were "indecent," that is, prostitutes who sold sex for money. The idea of sexually self-directed women was unheard-of in Europe. In stark contrast, Southeastern Native women had many options, including the right to have sex with anyone they chose.

In the late seventeenth and early eighteenth centuries, Native women often traveled with the *coureurs-de-bois* (French trappers), sometimes marrying them. In particular, Indian "hunting women" would accompany the French fur trappers, acting as interpreters, cooking, making clothing, cutting wood, and hauling water. In return, the men provided food, skins, and physical protection. More often than not, if they so desired, these hunting "wives" had sexual relations with the *coureurs-de-bois*, as well. In fact, it was the French traders who often needed the protection of the women's clan and nation, so there was reciprocity in these relationships based on mutual needs.

In other words, choice and direction in sexual relationships resided in the women. Southeastern women chose the men they wanted to have sexual relations with; the men did not choose them, for the freedom to choose was a woman's absolute right. Whereas the hunting wife was an institution throughout the Eastern woodlands, it had absolutely no counterpart in European culture.

Unmarried Native women also had the right to control their own fertility. They did not have to marry any man, nor was unmarried pregnancy considered immoral. The focus was on the child, not how it came to be, and every child was a sacred gift, not only to the mother but also to her clan. There was no stigma in having an "illegitimate" child, for in the non-Christian matriarchies of the Southeast, there was no such notion as bastardy. In fact, the free mating of the hunting wife was how the *Métis* Nation of Canada came to be. After the Treaty of Paris of 1763, which ended French colonialism in North America (not to be confused with the 1783 Treaty of Paris, which ended the American Revolution), many of the French returned to France, leaving their *Métis*, or mixed-blood, children with their Native mothers, creating the modern *Métis* nation. (*Métis* is French for "half.").

Once the British gained more control over "the colonies," Christian missionaries immediately began imposing their values regarding chastity, marriage, and morality on Southeastern women, in particular. The patriarchal society of the British dictated that men would be economically and socially dominant in this new land. Men, of course, were allowed to enjoy the double standard that was, well, *standard* in Europe. In addition to English moral standards, especially in the area of sexuality, the English language was imposed, as well. Subordinate and less powerful nations met with extinction under British rule, but fighting for their continued existence, broken clans began regrouping and consolidating with one another under the ancient Native adoption laws.

Once their self-determination had been compromised, Southeastern peoples were denied political and economic power. Their land was taken, and their population decreased dramatically as a result of warfare, genocide, and disease, three components so mixed together that, sometimes, it is hard to sort them out from one another. Indian losses only intensified after the American Revolution, when the "Treaty Period" of Native history began under the new U.S. government. Imposed political, religious, economic, and marriage systems greatly changed the social order and the status of Southeastern women.

It is axiomatic that women hold the greatest power in societies where they are the economic producers exercising some control over the distribution of economic resources. Once English-style capitalism replaced Native communalism, however, the trade-and-barter society (or, more accurately, the gifting economies) of Southeastern peoples shifted to the cash economy of the United States. Native women could no longer trade but instead had to buy. Worst of all, as the Euro-Americans imposed their notion of "private property" and began buying instead of using land, British-style common law kicked in with its notion of land ownership, a punitive legal system, a penal code, and male-dominated courts of law.

The resultant economic shift inflicted serious damage on the Southeastern matriarchies, especially as the women lost their ancient right to the land. Both the economic trauma and the sociopolitical disruption being visited on the Southeast worked against matriarchy. By forcing an entirely new system on Southeastern Natives, the British system managed to replace the more progressive Southeastern lifeways with its own, regressive ways.

As Native women saw their social and economic control slipping away, some noticed their political power was also at risk. By 1700, Native women who had enjoyed positions of leadership and equality were now experiencing the double jeopardy of being both discriminated against as women and treated unjustly as Natives by the newly arrived Euro-Americans. The harmony, cooperation, sharing, and generosity that characterized the Southeastern matriarchies gave way to internal colonialism.

Under Robert Blauner's theory, there are four basic characteristics of internal colonialism:

1. The colonized have a new social system imposed on them.
2. The Native culture is modified or destroyed.
3. The internal colony is controlled from the outside.
4. Racism prevails.[2]

All of these characteristics were present in the colonies by 1750.

After the American Revolution began in 1775, the political system of the United States changed from British colonial rule to the new, state-run "democracy" of America. For all the high-flown talk, however, the systems put in place by the Euro-Americans did not really change from those in place under the British. What did change was the political egalitarianism of the Southeast. Southeastern values were replaced with the invaders' values, Blauner's first and second stages of colonialism.

To understand how much was lost politically, it is first necessary to understand what once existed. In most cases, women in Southeastern cultures were noncombatants, but female fighters did exist, like Muscogee Coosaponakeesa ("Creek Mary"), who led her people in a successful campaign against the British in Savannah during the 1750s. Similarly, Cherokee Clan Mothers had the right to call and wage war. The office of *Da'nawagasta*, or "Sharp War," was held by a woman warrior who headed a women's military society. Women of influence, such as Coosaponakeesa, were harder to find in the late eighteenth century, after colonialism took firm hold.

Cherokee women also had the right to decide the fate of war captives, life-or-death decisions that were made by vote of the Women's Council and relayed to the district at large by the "War Woman," also known as the "Pretty Woman." Any decision over adoption had to be made by female clan heads, because a captive chosen to live was then adopted into one of the families, whose affairs were directed by the Clan Mothers.

The War Woman carried the title of Beloved Woman, and her power was great. The Women's Council, as distinguished from the district, village, or confederacy councils, was powerful in a number of political and sociospiritual ways. It may have had the deciding voice regarding which males served on the councils. Certainly the Women's Council was influential in national decisions, and its spokeswomen served as War Woman and Peace Woman, presumably holding offices in the towns designated as red towns (War) and white towns (Peace), respectively. Their other powers included the right to speak in the men's council, the right to choose whom and whether to marry, the right to bear arms, and the right to choose their extramarital occupations.[3] Under colonialism, the highly respected, political role of the Cherokees' Beloved Women sadly eroded.

Southeasterners recognized that the dramatic shifts in culture post-contact were related to the lack of power held by English women in their own society. Southeastern Natives even commented on it. In fact, Atagulkalu (Attakullaculla, "Leaning Wood"), a Cherokee diplomat who had spent time in England negotiating an agreement with King George II, called the British on their failure to include women in their councils in 1757.[4] The British turned away from his plea to include women, puzzled rather than enlightened. Due to this oblivion, the British were unable to grasp that Southeastern women held key roles as decision makers and consequently denied them any power to make decisions under colonial rule.

Native self-determination had been slipping away throughout the eighteenth century due to European imperialism. For instance, when the French left the county after the Treaty of Paris was signed in 1763, they ceded southern Alabama to England and Louisiana to Spain.

Natives were never mentioned in or consulted for that first Treaty of Paris. Southeastern Natives believed that the Europeans were, thereby, dividing and ceding land that had never been European in the first place. All of the land involved was Native American land, yet they were powerless to stop the paper transfers of land.

The erosion of the power of Native women continued as the American Revolution toppled the major Southeastern nations. In 1775, after the Revolution had begun, European settlers believed that *all* the land, North and South, belonged rightfully to them. Native people did not see it that way. In most cases, Native Americans had not relinquished rights to their land, nor had they been defeated by the British or the Americans, both of whom claimed it. Certainly, nations like the Seminoles were not ready to concede anything to any European seizure.

Immediately after the Revolution, with its British concession of "the Northwest Territories" (Ohio, Michigan, Indiana, Illinois, and Wisconsin) at the 1783 Treaty of Paris, the new American government began the process of "removing" Indians to Ohio, the first dumping ground of the first removals, so that white settlers could move in. The settlers resorted to:

1. Warfare,
2. Organized raids on Indian settlements,
3. Blatant massacres, and
4. The destruction of the ecological base of Native survival.[5]

The Revolution brought chaos to Native Americans, both North and South. The new United States tried to rationalize its conquest and subjugation of Native people by posing as the benefactor and guardian of Indian people. The new Americans put forth the notion that uncivilized, non-christian Natives were incapable of caring for themselves but needed guidance to create "civilized" societies. The marginalization of the matriarchy was now complete. Outside of their national community, no one in power was even aware of the lost cultural tradition of matriarchy.

While claiming to be the guardian of Native Americans and their interests, the U.S. government crafted policies, laws, and cultural frameworks that were to demolish what was left of the matriarchies of the so-called Five Civilized Tribes of the Southeast: the Muscogee, the Choctaw, the Chickasaw, the Cherokee, and the newly formed Seminole Nation, which consisted of Muscogees allied with escaped African slaves. These actions by the United States also led to the largest land grab in American history.

The Red Stick Creeks, who were followers of Tecumseh, fought U.S. troops at Horseshoe Bend in 1813. After Tecumseh was killed, the survivors, known as Refugee Creeks, retreated to Spanish Florida. The Seminoles fought the longest war with the United States, from 1817 intermittently through 1842. They were never defeated. Andrew Jackson, so instrumental in the early wars against Southeastern nations, then pressed his genocidal policies by enforcing the Indian Removal Act (1830), authorizing the Bureau of Indian Affairs (BIA) to relocate all Eastern Natives west of the Mississippi River. Any nation that attempted to resist was to be relocated by military force.

All five of the large nations of the Southeast were removed at tremendous costs in lives and real dollars. The U.S. Army protected the rights of white settlers to take Native land, whereas the rights of Natives did not exist. In despair, the great nations of the American Southeast faced Removal, one after another, to "Indian Territory," a place the Choctaws called "home of the red man," or Oklahoma. By the lowest estimates, 25 percent of the population of each nation forced onto its particular "Trail of Tears" died of disease, exposure, and malnutrition en route. Approximately 50 percent of the entire Cherokee population—8,000 people—died during the forced march, most of the dead being women and children. The Choctaws' forced removal from Mississippi in 1836 was equally devastating, involving the loss of 15 percent of their population, or 6,000 out of 40,000 people. The Chickasaw suffered severe loses, as well. By contrast, the Muscogees and Seminoles are said to have suffered about a 50 percent mortality. For the Muscogees, this came primarily in the period immediately after Removal. For example, of the 10,000 or more of those who were resettled from 1836 to 1837, an incredible 3,500 died of bilious fevers.[6]

The Removal controversy dominated Native–settler relations from the 1820s until the Civil War began in 1861. Native men stood as the treaty signers, so that Southeastern women's former role as political equals and wartime decision makers, not to mention proprietors of the land, was denied to them. Importantly, traditionalists who did not sign remained at home, cherishing older ways that recognized women. Thus, for all of the federal muscle used in trying to force Southeastern peoples off their land, remnant bands of every nation escaped Removal, remaining in their traditional homelands, living in traditional ways. In the twenty-first century, the Cherokees, Choctaws, Muscogees, and Seminoles still have communities and a few reservations in their home-lands. To this day, remnant groups of Yuchi, Chickasaws, and others remain hidden in Mississippi, Tennessee, and elsewhere.

Wherever the survivors were, the psychological and spiritual scars of the Trail of Tears passed from one generation to the next. Now, such suffering is called intergenerational trauma, but although the suffering has been named, no restitution has been made for it. The U.S. gov-ernment has never taken responsibility for the atrocities it committed against America's indigenous people. Instead, all that was ever received by way of an apology for Removal was lamely offered in September of 2000 by the then-head of the BIA, Kevin Gover, himself a Pawnee—an irony not lost on Indians.

Removal hardly ended the assault on Native self-determination. The lands in Indian Territory designated for the Five Civilized Tribes were manipulated into ever-smaller parcels by the government. This was because the government was taking away land promised the South-eastern Natives to give to other Natives being removed from other places in the East. When the Chickasaws arrived in Indian Territory, for instance, they bought land from their closest relatives, the Choc-taws. Similarly, when the Seminoles arrived, they were given land bought from the Creeks. The land base of Indian Territory continued to shrink, as the Cherokees took in the Lenapes ("Delawares") in 1867 and the Shawnees in 1870. Some of the Catawbas, or eastern Lakotas, came to live with the Choctaws in 1871. The Caddos from Texas fled brutal treatment by coming on their own to Indian Territory. Each new arrival crowded the landscape. Importantly, Indian Territory was under the complete control of the federal government. Women were hardly even a blip on its radar.

In 1866, new treaties were imposed on the nations that fought on the side of the Confederacy during the Civil War, punishing them for fighting on the "wrong side." The western half of Indian Territory was thus taken away from the Confederate Choctaws, Chickasaws, and Cherokees, who had followed General Stan Watie of the Cherokees, the only Native General in the Confederacy, who led his all-Native division. Even as land was stripped from Confederate Natives, other Native land was being taken for the transcontinental railroads. Finally, because the U.S. government really had no plan for what to do with the Freedmen, or freed slaves, many were to made citizens of the "Indian" nations and consequently allowed to claim land in "Indian Territory."[7] Every successive adjustment to laws or treaties led to smaller land holdings by the five large nations of the Southeast.

Having acquired nearly all of the Indian land holdings and confined Natives to reservations by 1871, Congress tired of making treaties with them. There really being no Natives left to contend the point effectively, Congress unilaterally ended the practice of treating with them. For their part, Southeastern Natives felt that the end was long overdue. Aside from the fact that nearly all extant treaties were fraudulent, none of the provisions of the 364 treaties with the Natives was ever honored by the U.S. government, anyway.

The next hundred years of Indian and U.S. government relations involved one failed program after another. The Dawes Act of 1887 intended to destroy the Native communities by dividing up and allotting 40 to 160 acres of land to individual Indian head of households. The "excess" land could then be sold to the settlers, and Indians would then become the holders of "private property," like their Euro-American neighbors. This was an assimilation tactic that was not only unsuccessful but also resulted in many Natives losing their allotted land. Because the concept of taxing land was foreign, Natives did not pay their property taxes and wound up forfeiting their land for back taxes.

More importantly, as an addendum to Dawes, the U.S. government passed a law in 1888 that declared that all Native women marrying Euro-American men had de facto agreed to abandon their Native identity.[8] Not only they but all their children lost their right to be Natives and live as Natives. This law hit Southeastern Native women very hard. A primary tactic for separating Natives from their land was for a settler man to marry a woman from one of the Five Civilized Tribes. He thereby gained her land because, under Euro-American law, the wife's property passed to her husband.

From 1871 until the present, then, nothing in the U.S. treatment of Indians has improved the status of Indian women. Consider the following "failed experiments":

- Federal suppression of Native American religion until the passage of the Indian Freedom of Religion Act of 1978 finally gave Indians the same rights to their beliefs that all other Americans have. Under this policy, Southeastern women were not only denied their spiritual traditions, but also their strong place as leaders in and practitioners of their traditional belief systems. Euro-American religion had no leadership roles for women.

- Indian children being taken from their families and placed in boarding schools to "save the child, but kill the Indian." This policy resulted in untold physical, psychological, and sexual abuse of female and male Native children.[9] The boarding schools contributed to the destruction of Native parents, families, and nations. The problems around parenting issues in Indian country today are a direct result of the Indian Boarding School era, which began in 1879 with the Carlisle Indian School and continues in a limited way up to the present. The trauma induced by this system contributed to the rise in alcoholism, suicide, and mental illness still prevalent in Indian country today.[10] Women bear the social brunt of these ills.

- Injustices such as the nonconsensual sterilization by the Indian Health Service of 40 percent of Native women of childbearing age without their knowledge, a practice that continued through the 1970s. The U.S. population control policy amounted to genocide by any standards.[11]

- Removal of Indian children from their families and placement in foster care. Estimates suggest that as many as 30 percent of all Indian children have been removed from their homes.[12]

• Shocking disparities in the area of health care. Compared to the mainstream population of the United States, Native Americans are more than
four times as likely to die from diabetes; six times as likely to die from
tuberculosis; and more than seven times as likely to die from alcoholism.
Natives have a suicide rate four times the national average.[13]

Native women have been those most affected by all these impositions of colonialism. First and foremost, Southeastern women have
seen their matriarchy destroyed. As women, they once had all the
rights and powers that American women today are struggling to obtain,
including economic and political power; spiritual equality; the right to
proper health care, up to and including abortion on demand; the right
to divorce on demand; and the right to call—and call off—war.

In 1986, Margaret Schuler summarized some of the major categories
of human rights violations that frequently affect women:[14]

1. Economic exploitation (no minimum wage laws and no day care rights),
2. Lack of equal treatment of women by family law systems,
3. Denial of reproductive rights (including the right to contraceptive information, medically safe abortions, and the right to bear or not bear
   children), and
4. Violence and exploitation (including domestic violence, rape, sexual
   harassment, sex trafficking, and coerced prostitution).

Consistent with Schuler's findings, Indian women lack any sort of
economic clout. According to the U.S. Department of Labor, unemployment for Native women in 1995 stood at 14.4 percent.[15] Because
unemployment and poverty accompany each other, the national poverty
rate for Native Americans was 24.5 percent in 2001.[16] Poverty and
unemployment tend to entrap Native women when they find themselves
in violent and abusive situations, as they very often do.

Among a population that is already reeling from unequal and inadequate health care, Native women find themselves at high risk for health-
related problems from diabetes, heart disease, and diabetic eye disease to
HIV/AIDS and cancer. Thus, not only have 40 percent of living Native

women been sterilized without their consent, but even those still fertile are so wracked by disease and poor health care that their chances of producing healthy offspring are minimized. Furthermore, they have much less time to give to a family. Whereas the average life expectancy for Euro-American women is eighty-one years, Native American women can expect to live little more than half that, or fifty-two years.

Native women are also victimized at alarming rates. According to statistics from the U.S. Department of Justice in 2004, Native American females are two and a half times more likely to be victims of a violent crime than any other group of females in the United States.[17] In 70 percent of these attacks, Native American female victims reported the attacker was either white or black. In cases of rape or sexual assault, Native victims reported that the offender was Euro-American in four out of five attacks. Unlike other groups of victims, they were more likely to be attacked by a stranger than an intimate partner, family member, or acquaintance, a circumstance that is virtually unheard of in crime statistics elsewhere. Finally, even though Native women make up 0.6 percent of the U.S. population, 1.5 percent of victims of violence are Indian women.[18]

These statistics can only mean that Native American women are the culturally designated victims, par excellence, of internal colonialism. Instead of the power brokers they were even two hundred years ago, Native women today are economically, socially, spiritually, and politically broken. They form a silent, marginalized, and oppressed minority, dependent upon equally dispossessed male partners for survival. The European model for this marginalization is so antiquated that not even Euro-American conservatives follow it. Although the regression is rarely discussed or noted in mainstream society, the position of Indian women in American society has regressed to the point that they suffer the lowest economic, educational, and social status of *any* group in American society.

Clearly, the matriarchy has fallen, and the losers are all of us—Euro-American, African American, Asian American, and latino/a, as well as Native American. The vibrant model of matriarchy posed by Native women of the Southeast was rooted out precisely because of the threat that it offered the Euro-Christian model of hierarchical patriarchy.

Now that the rest of the world has finally caught up with what Southeastern Indians knew all along, is it not time that the women of the Southeast regained their status as full members of the human community?

NOTES

1. Mark Van Doren (ed.), *Travels of William Bartram* (1791; New York: Dover, 1955), p. 252.

2. Robert Blauner, *Racial and Ethnic Groups in America*, 3rd ed. (Dubuque, IA: Kendall Hunt, 1969), p. 15.

3. S. C. Williams (ed.), *Lieutenant Henry Timberlake's Memoirs, 1756–1765* (1927, reprint; Marietta, GA: Continental Book, 1948), p. 94.

4. Alice Beck Kehoe, *North American Indians: A Comprehensive Account*, 2nd ed. (Englewood Cliffs, NJ: Prentice Hall, 1992), p. 203.

5. Vine Deloria Jr., *Custer Died for Your Sins: An Indian Manifesto* (New York: Avon, 1969), pp. 61–63; Barbara Alice Mann, "The Greenville Treaty of 1795: Pen-and-Ink Witchcraft in the Struggle for the Old Northwest," in Bruce E. Johansen (ed.), Enduring *Legacies: Native American Treaties and Contemporary Controversies* (Westport, CT: Praeger, 2004), pp. 136–201.

6. Russell Thornton, "Cherokee Population Losses during the Trail of Tears: A New Perspective and a New Estimate," *Ethnohistory* 31 (1984): p. 291.

7. Kehoe, *North American Indians*, p. 199; Barbara Alice Mann, "'A Man of Misery': Chitto Harjo and the Senate Select Committee on Oklahoma Statehood," in Barbara Alice Mann (ed.), *Native American Speakers of the Eastern Woodlands: Selected Speeches and Critical Analyses* (Westport, CT: Greenwood, 2001), pp. 197–228. The classic source on this issue is Angie Debo, *And Still the Waters Run: The Betrayal of the Five Civilized Tribes*, 4th ed. (Princeton, NJ: Princeton University Press, 1991).

8. An Act in Relation to Marriage between White Men and Indian Women, 25 Stat. L., 392, 9 August 1888.

9. For an intensive look at boarding school problems, see *Native Americas* (Winter 2000). Most of the issue is dedicated to the boarding school experience. See Darren Bonaparte, "Running for Safety," *Native Americas* (Winter 2000): 15 for sexual abuse.

10. Ron Lewis and M. K. Ho, "Social Work with Native Americans," *Social Work* (September 1975): pp. 379–382.

11. Jim Vander Wall, "American Indian Women at the Center of the Indigenous Resistance in Contemporary North America," in M. Annette Jaimes (ed.), *The State of Native America: Genocide, Colonization and Resistance* (Boston: South End Press, 1992), p. 326; Sally S. Torphy, "Native American Women and Coerced Sterilization: On the Trail of Tears in the 1970's," *American Indian Cultures and Research Journal* 24, no. 2 (2000): pp. 1–22.

12. Terry Cross, *Indian Child Welfare Report* (Portland, OR: Indian Child Welfare Association, 2002), p. 6.

13. Rachel Joseph, "Indian Health Care Improvement Act Reauthorization Amendments of 2004," Hearing on SB 212/ HR 2440 before the House Resources Committee, 107th Congress, Testimony of Rachel Joseph, Cochair, National Steering Committee, 2004, p. 127.

14. Margaret Schuler, "Women and the Law," in R. S. Gallin, M. Aronoff, and A. Ferguson (eds.), *Women and International Development*, Annual vol. 1 (Boulder, CO: Westview Press: 1986): pp. 155–187.

15. U.S. Department of Labor, Bureau of Indian Affairs, *1995 Annual Report, Quiet Crisis: Federal Funding and Un-met Needs in Indian Country* (Washington, DC: Government Printing Office, 2003), p. 32.

16. U.S. Census Bureau, *Poverty in the United States: 2001: Current Population Reports* (Washington, DC: Government Printing Office, 2002), p. 7.

17. U.S. Department of Justice, Bureau of Statistics, *American Indians and Crime* (Washington, DC: Bureau of Justices Statistics Clearinghouse, 2004), p. 1.

18. Ibid., p. 7.

CHAPTER 4

Slow Runners

~

Barbara Alice Mann

In May 2005, when I mentioned to a Native American colleague from west of the Mississippi River that I had just published *George Washington's War on Native America*, she responded, "Oh, that old stuff. It doesn't matter much out here." I was dumbfounded, for, in the Eastern woodlands, the American Revolution is a major historical benchmark, designated *Hanötaká:nyas*, "The Holocaust," by the Iroquois, long before the same word was siphoned off to indicate the Jewish Shoah.[1]

Nothing could better encapsulate the mismatch of mindsets between Natives east and west of the Mississippi River than this little exchange. For the most part, Western Natives are fairly unaware of the deep and fraught history of the East, tending to see it as just the unredacted version of their own ninety-year face-off with invasion and conquest. By and large, they assume that their compressed version speaks more efficiently to the subject than Algonkin traditions that start with Verrazano's 1524 harrassment of the Eastern seaboard or the Shawnee traditions of the first Spaniards in the late 1490s, let alone Wampanoag traditions that begin with the Viking invasion of 1000.

The breezy dismissal of our extended tussle with the Europeans does a serious disservice to Eastern nations for during this time, the Northeastern Iroquois League, in particular, frustrated and obstructed settler efforts to push westward. It is, in fact, largely thanks to the dogged opposition of League peoples that the settlers did not mass in the Upper Great Lakes, their gateway into the Plains and points West, before 1830. The intense resistance to invasion by the Iroquois spared their Lakes, Plains, Southwestern, and Northwestern cousins three hundred years worth of additional suffering.

In accomplishing this notable feat, League peoples endured waves of genocidal attacks that became downright annual, from the mid-1600s through to the death of Tecumseh in 1813. Families regularly faced flight, the refugees running from desperation to despair, with the homicidal militias hot on their rear. Decade after decade, the Iroquois outlasted famines wrought by the destruction of their sustaining crops courtesy of those same militias, enraged not to have caught their shivering prey. Year upon year, Iroquoian peoples watched beloved lives lost to serial murder, their children's hair ripped off for the omnipresent scalp bounties offered by settler governments, whose premiums counted a child of ten as an adult.[2]

All of these struggles occurred *before* Jacksonian Removal, the only Eastern benchmark that most Western Natives know of. Out West, "The Last of the Mahicans" is a misspelled book title, not the living tradition of the March 8, 1782, militia massacre of ninety-six innocents at Goschochking, Ohio.[3] Ground into inattention by their own miseries, Western Natives are so unaware of the taut history of their Eastern cousins that many even flatly deny us existence in the present.

Both the ignorance and the denial echo settler fictions. The media has annointed the Lakota culture THE Native culture, so that tipis and sundances are prerequisities of Indian identity in the popular American mind. Female-led, constitutional democracies fed by large-scale, women-run agriculture ring no bells of recognition for either the general public or Western Natives. So completely disregarded has Eastern culture been, that I actually know some Western Natives who dragged the White Buffalo Calf Woman to Ohio, fully expecting her to resonate with woodlanders here. When I took up a collection of gas money, to help WBCW get back home, they were affronted, not amused. Their consciousness remained unraised.

Worse, media-fed projections of the Lakotas as iconic confuse wellmeaning but hapless Eastern Natives into copying the traditions and ways of the Lakotas, in the name of recovering Eastern cultures. The result of their "Pan-Indianism," better described as Lakota Lite™, is quite dire, for the spirits of place do not recognize, nor do they know what to do with, ritual practices developed elsewhere. This is not a minor issue. The spirits are real, and so is their medicine. It has a genuine effect, and, as every decent medicine person knows, a disastrous one, should hacks or novices fling it about, carelessly mixing and matching practices in the Pan-Indian way—a chunk of Lakota here and a dollop of Abenaki there, with a smidgen of Squamish squirted over the top.

Consider the Pan-Indian use of eagle feathers by both men and women to confer speaking rights. Nothing could be farther from the Eastern interface with eagle feathers. In the first place, eagles are important Sky medicine, which puts them exclusively in the realm of *male* medicine. Second, ritual eagle feathers are kill-medicine when waved about in front of groups. Only qualified medicine men may safely handle eagle feathers at all, and, if they do it in public, someone had better hide. Consequently, in the East, traditional women do not handle eagle feathers. If a woman has such a feather, something seriously nasty is afoot. An Eastern Clan Mother pointing an eagle feather at another woman is committing an assault against her. It is the direct equivalent of a man publicly throwing a bloody menstrual rag on another man. Nevertheless, so pervasive is Pan-Indianism, on the one hand, and so little known are real Eastern traditions on the other, that well-meaning, if untaught, Eastern women walk around with eagle feathers drooping from their belts, wondering why their "luck" is so bad.

Such insensitivity is not the fault of Western Indians but of the U.S. government, which assured Western peoples that their Eastern cousins were all dead, an obituary that Western Natives readily believed, in light of their own ungentle experience with the settlers. Consequently, more than one west-of-the-Mississippi Indian has blithely assured me to my face that if any Natives are still in the East, they "lost their culture," long ago. Most Western Natives are openly skeptical when informed that, nope, Eastern Indians are alive and well. Indeed, so firmly do they believe that Eastern Indians are all deceased, that reservation councils have taken to banishing undesirable elements East, especially to those the nineteen states with no reservations, places that Western Natives consider "No Man's Land" but we consider "Home."

With mounting dismay, I have witnessed a parade of off-reservation miscreants storming onto Eastern lands, using their federal cards to pass go, collect, two hundred dollars and get out of jail free, all the while leaving mud trails of chaos in their wake. Instead of presenting themselves to the general public as what they are, unwanted, uninvited, and unmannerly interlopers, they pose for press photos as Real Deal Indians. Typically knowing little about their own cultures—and, even more typically, nothing whatsoever about *Eastern* cultures—they berate Non-Treaty (i.e., unenrolled) Indians as frauds, including locally revered elders and medicine workers. In the East, where the harshest repudiation allowed in public is to state of someone, "We do not know that person," these wild accusations are not only astoundingly rude, but they are also doing East–West relations untold harm.

The actual problem here is not that Western nations are imperialistic monsters, but that the U.S. government is undermining respect for traditional self-determination. A nonindigenous player, the federal government confers artificial status on Indians coming from outside the natural polities of Eastern nations. Because of the benighted way that the laws were conceived, federal recognition empowers anyone, from anywhere, no matter how low his or her status may be at home, to dictate policy in Eastern groups, just so long as she waves about a federal enrollment card first. This creates competing authorities, with the U.S. government tipping the balance. Federal recognition thus upends traditional Eastern systems by allowing enrolled outsiders to impose their agendas on Eastern groups through grand-standing and floor-grabbing.

Traditionally, Eastern nations are very careful about who speaks, and in which councils. We have formally appointed speakers who air predetermined arguments through appropriate channels. Before taking the floor, legitimate speakers to a council are expected to produce wampum given them by their Clan Mothers, thus demonstrating not just their office as speakers but also which entity sent them.

This procedure signals that their message is legitimate. There are, moreover, very specific rules governing visitation, and, before federal impositions, anyway, strangers were strictly held to them. If a troublemaker from outside the clan or nation attempted to enter its domain and hold forth, female clan councils, and male national councils, put an immediate stop to the interference by sending official speakers to put three direct questions to the interloper:

1. Who are your elders?
2. What message did they give you for us?
3. What Clan Mother welcomed you, strange person?

These were not rhetorical questions but required literal answers. A loud-mouthed upstart who had not been sent by his or her elders with a real message and who had not, furthermore, been welcomed by a recognized local Clan Mother, was simply not listened to. We did not know that person, so no such visitor had rights of entry to, let alone of speaking in, any council. The best he or she could expect was temporary lodging in a "stranger house" and the gift of new moccasins and enough food to enable him or her to make the journey back home. In other words, self-appointed speakers were sent packing.[1] These laws allowed local communities to control entry into their public forum and thereby determine their own agendas.

Under federal systems now in place, however, whether banished or not, More-Indian-Than-Thou interlopers impose themselves upon local councils, often seizing the "right" to dictate policies and goals. They not infrequently use their insider access to set up "Indian programs." (For whom, I always wonder, all those Eastern Natives they claim do not exist?) These programs poverty-pimp for all they are worth, looking to get us poor Eastern slobs mentally healthy, sober, on welfare, or all of the above. Apparently unaware that *powwow* is a Narrangansett term meaning medicine person, or that Buffalo Bill Cody invented the current powwow format by including "savage" dancing in his Wild West Show, they fundraise through powwows that always showcase

Western fancy-dancers to the exclusion of Eastern dance styles. As shills for the racist stereotype of Indians as feckless, reckless, dancing drunks, these programs do a great job. At last notice, however, they address none of the front-burner issues on Eastern agendas: recognition of the rights of Non-Treaty Peoples, repatriation of human remains and grave goods, land re/acquisition, language revitalization, and mound preservation, especially of sacred sites.

For about twenty-five years, I was too floored by the warped cruelty of federal myths and the intimidation tactics of the Identity Police to object, but since then, I have gathered myself up sufficiently to challenge both forms of bullying. My purpose in doing so is not to wedge Eastern and Western Natives farther apart, but to introduce sanity to the subject by forging bonds of mutual respect and cooperation between the cousined halves, thus recreating the Native whole that animated Turtle Island before she was invaded by Europeans. Our proper task is to heal the unnatural rifts caused by colonialism and its descendant, federalism, not to collaborate with Department of the Interior, which groups Natives along with flora and fauna to issue them what amount to dog tags.

My first order of business is to point out that the charge of "lost culture" arises, not from any Native inspection of the issue, but rather from nineteenth-century federal court decrees. In anticipation of the Dawes Act (which was in agitation as early as 1883),[5] the courts deliberately sought to cut Eastern Natives off from their Western kinfolk as damage control once Dawes enrollment was imposed. Part of the Dawes plan was to allot land to Natives, and officials wanted to prevent any of that land from being claimed east of the Mississippi. Consequently, in 1885, the U.S. Court of Claims sneered at Eastern Natives as decultured refuse; in 1886, the U.S. Supreme Court reiterated and legitimated that stance, so that it became a common federal refrain.

Moving first on the issue in 1885, the Court of Claims indicated that it knew perfectly well that Non-Treaty Peoples remained in the East but contended that the United States needed neither to recognize nor to deal with those nations—in this instance, specifically the Cherokees—claiming that they were "but a social organization," for:

No treaty was ever made with this band nor with the people composing its membership. All the connection the band has with the United States is such as has been created by the laws of Congress, which may be altered by the same power than enacted them; and Congress can make no laws in relation to the band which are in conflict with the laws and constitution of the State of North Carolina, to which these Indians are subject.[6]

Following suit in 1886, the Supreme Court simultaneously recognized but rejected Eastern Non-Treaty Peoples, adding rather nastily that their lack of federal recognition was their own, dad-gummed fault for not cooperating with Removal: "The Cherokees in North Carolina dissolved their connection with their Nation when they refused to accompany the body of it on its removal, and they have had no separate political organization since. Whatever union they have had among themselves has been merely a social or business one."[7]

The precedent was thus set by the time of Judge William D. Springer's 1898 decision barring Eastern Indians from Dawes enrollment, again in particular reference to the Cherokees but with general application to all Eastern Natives. Springer was simply repeating the, by then commonplace, assertion that Eastern nations were "mere social organizations." Because Eastern Natives had deliberately "expatriated themselves" from the transported portion of their nations during Jacksonian Removal, he ruled, they deserved no further consideration as Natives.[8] Citing Removal "treaties," federal courts generally began pretending that the Indians, themselves, agreed with this fiction. Jacksonian Removal was forced, however, and its treaties were *never* agreed to by large segments of the removed nations, many of whom remained in the East as Non-Treaty Peoples.

These court decisions thus first denied Eastern Natives unity and culture, and second, claimed that permanent separation from their kinsfolk was a consciously intended result on their part of evading Jacksonian Removal. Skewed to facilitate land theft under the Dawes Act and offered damagingly from the settler-centric point of view, these rulings typify what Northeastern peoples have traditionally called "pen-and-ink witchcraft," that is, making paper say what reality never said, and thereafter using the paper version as a substitute for the truth.[9]

On the contrary, the East-West separation was instigated by the double-barreled Removal Act of 1830, which sought to prop up the U.S. economy by appropriating valuable Native lands in the East, while at the same time eliminating the safe haven of Eastern Indian culture, to which all too many African slaves had been escaping. The federal courts certainly knew this history in 1898, when Springer flatly declared Eastern peoples non-Natives, for the Cherokees had valiantly fought Removal all the way to the Supreme Court, even winning their case by having Removal declared unconstitutional, only to be removed, anyway, in the criminal round-ups ordered by President Andrew Jackson.

Consequently, whether or not they know it, by parroting the slur that Eastern Natives have "lost their culture," Western Natives are simply aiding the government's very political purpose of "disappearing" Eastern Natives through "documentary genocide," that is, by killing people on paper, when they are not in fact dead.[10] To dispel the miasma here, I ask Western Indians to recall the last time that the federal government told them the truth about Native American history. Once they realize that the answer is "never," I would request them to reconsider echoing that deeply flawed source any further concerning their Eastern cousins.

Far from "mere social groups," Eastern fires comprise the descendants of diehard resisters, ancestors who bravely remained East despite Jacksonian Removal, at a time when settlers construed evading Removal as an act of war punishable by death. By and large, these Longhairs were the last hold-outs of the Black Drink Resistance that flourished in the East from before the *first* Removal of the late 1790s through to the second, Jacksonian, Removal from 1828 to 1845.[11] The Black Drink Resistance was carried to Indian Territory, by the way, so that most Western Natives know it as the Four Mothers Resistance, which sought to incorporate Indian Territory into the Native-run State of Sequoyah, in the attempt to block its settler takeover as "Oklahoma" in 1907.[12]

The loss of Tecumseh in 1813 was a serious blow to the original Black Drink Resistance but not its death knell in the East. Especially in Ohio, the cradle of resistance from 1783 on, such important nineteenth-century leaders as Teökwe't ("Deunquat," "Deunkwat," "He Is Human") and Hë:töh ("Hetlo," "Hitlo," "Hilo," "He Is the Leader") continued locally resisting invasion and forced assimilation after the flawed Greenville Treaty was signed in 1795.[13] In the 1820s, Teökwe't brilliantly disrupted the Methodist missionaries, the advance guard of the settlers then staking out the valuable Sandusky region, while Hë:töh, my direct ancestor, led Seneca families into the Great Black Swamp in northwest Ohio, there to hide from Ohio Removal in the mid-1840s. The Odawas of the Three Fires Confederacy led similar resistance elements to Walpole Island, Canada, where they remain to this day. In the South, holed up along the Ohio River, were the Cherokees in the Appalachian hills and the Shawnees in the swamps of the Big and Little Miami Rivers. Lenapes and Mahicans similarly hid out, in the southeastern Appalachians. These were Non-Treaty Peoples, holdouts who flatly refused to recognize land-stripping treaties or to attend (and thereby legitimize) the councils that negotiated them.

None of these Non-Treaty Indians "lost their culture." Far from it, they risked everything to remain free in their homelands, tending ceremonially to the graves of their ancestors, feeding the Spirits of Earth and Sky, and holding onto ancient customs. Indeed, where the old ways were lost, and soon, was on reservations, whose Indian agents and missionaries could tyrannize captive audiences into assimilation.

At least in Ohio—the Indian Territory of the first Removal of the late 1790s—far from lying around the fort, Indians were lying as low as possible. Demonstrably as many of them hid out as acceded to Jacksonian Removal, so that the Ohio Longhairs had a traditional name for those transported west: Slow Runners.[14] By and large, it was the most assimilated elements of the Eastern Natives who were removed because they were the cultural Slow Runners who had violated the two arch tenets of the Black Drink Resistance:

1. Never to convert to Christianity, and
2. Never to allow their names to be "made dead bugs on bark," that is, recorded on missionary or governmental lists.

Not only did the Slow Runners have dead-bug names, but also—superficially, anyhow—they converted to Christianity. Both deeds made it easy for the settlers to round them up and ship them out, because the authorities knew exactly whom to find, where.

By contrast, resisters hid, often in plain sight, in their Eastern homelands. Furthermore, some of those transported West sneaked back home after 1850, their stories of horrendous suffering in tow, for the government promptly reneged on many of its promises of succor. In particular, christianized, treaty Wyandots from Ohio endured the miseries of Removal in 1845 only, for their pains, to be declared "white" by the governmental decree in 1855, thus obviating the federal obligation to provision them with resettlement aid.[15] Newly "white," part of these Wyandots returned to Ohio, bitterly renouncing Christianity to join the Longhairs. Others begged the Oklahoma Senecas to take them in, where their quantum counts started at zero—for, after all, they were "white" now.

Back East, Longhairs could hide in the coal-laden hills only as long as settlers did not appropriate them; swamps remained feasible hiding places only until the settlers drained them. In Ohio, the expropriation of Appalachia set to immediately following the Civil War, while in the 1890s, settlers tiled the massive Great Black Swamp, which occupied nearly all of northwest Ohio, thus draining that natural wonder of the world, a decidous wetland in northern latitudes. At that juncture, resisters were forced into open interaction with the settlers. The primary method Natives employed for staying alive was hiding in their skin, which meant altering dress and language so as to live as inconspicuously as possible along the fringes of settler society. I suspect that these low-profile tactics are what have confused Western Natives into assuming that the federal courts were right: Their Eastern cousins had, indeed, "lost their culture."

Plain-sight hiding was facilitated by a central fact that is, today, also held against Eastern, and especially Northeastern, Indians: their light skin tones. Here, more than anywhere else, popular illusion disfigures truth. The Hollywood stereotype of dark-skinned "savages" could not speak less to Northeastern realities. Nevertheless, no more immune to media imagery than Euro-Americans, Western Natives assume that, if

Eastern Natives are "white," they got that way through the "dilution" of intermarriage with Euro-Americans. Otherwise, their light skin is taken to mean that they are not actually Indian, at all.

These insidious, and disturbingly racist, perspectives swallow colonial blither whole rather than consult Eastern historical reality. The well-documented fact is that, not only Northeastern, but also several Southeastern groups, especially the Cherokees, were, *at contact*, white-skinned people.[16] Some were even blue-eyed, although more were grey-eyed. To this day, "Grey-Eyes" is a lineage name among the Ohio Iroquois (including former Ohioans, now in Oklahoma). This was not only an Eastern phenomenon. The Western Mandans were famously white-skinned, while the Lakotas are suspiciously light-skinned themselves. Hmmm.

Early Anglo-American scholars, racists all, knew this. Because light-skinned Natives undermined nineteenth-century "science" of race, those scholars worked doggedly to explain away Indian "whiteness." With straight faces, they posited:

- handsful of shipwrecked Europeans, staggering 500 miles inland to impregnate thousands of giddy Native girls, before disappearing from history without a trace;[17]
- Atlantean refugees (voted "white" on principle) likewise reeling inland, this time, a thousand miles, to build the mounds and procreate madly, before being wiped out of existence by the heinous "savages";[18]
- ancient Celtic princes and paupers hurrying over in the twelfth century to brighten up the landscape—just in the nick of time for "Discovery"—before expiring themselves, probably from sexual exhaustion;[19]
- or, hey, just about *anything* to lighten up the continental motherlode rather than admit that Europeans were far from the world's only "white" people.

As yet unburdened by colonial racism, which was not fully articulated until the late-eighteenth century, the first-contact French missionaries in the Northeast never stopped citing the fact of white-skinned, brown-haired, light-eyed Indians, because they considered it proof positive that French–Native intermarriage was not just palatable but also inviting. From 1610 to 1750, such mating violated none of the au courant rules of French colonialism, which viewed interracial marriage as just dandy, so long as conversion to Roman Catholicism accompanied it.

Politically, France licked its lips over the fact of white-skinned Natives, for that would allow France to secure its beachhead in Canada by promoting ever-popular family values, that is, by marrying its *coureurs-de-bois* (backwoodsmen) to Indian women. French Canadian *realpolitik* thus created the *Metís* (literally, "half-breed") Nation, now considered entirely Native by British Canadian law. This marry-'em tactic should not be construed to mean that French policy bleached out U.S. Natives, for it was unsuccessful south of the St. Lawrence River, due to the dedicated rejection of French rule by the Iroquois League. My point here is not French "tolerance," but the preexistence of white-skinned Natives that excited French settlement policies in the first place. League peoples were light-skinned before the French arrived and remained so after the French invasion, without so much as a howdy-do exchanged.

The supposed "color" of Eastern Natives reflected both deliberate tanning techniques and easy consort with escaped Africans. Artificial skin color was very popular among Northeastern Indians. In fact, woodlanders invented suntan lotion, which they used all summer long to repel insects and sunburn. These sweet-scented unguents, made from refined bear grease, were often mixed with red ochre, which by summer's end yielded the original copper-tone tan.[20] The French missionaries bemoaned the suntans because it undermined their settlement schemes. The French solution was to mimic elite behavior in Europe by keeping converts out of the sun, for "the Savages would be very white if they were well covered."[21]

The infusion of melanin reflects the Northeastern Native attitudes toward European chattel Slavery. The Iroquois League in particular denounced Slavery as an engine of colonialism and made a habit of giving safe haven to any escaped slaves who made it to Iroquoia. Especially in old Iroquoia (Ohio, western Pennsylvania, West Virginia, and New York), many escaped slaves were happily adopted into the clans, intermarrying and enjoying all the rights of Indian citizenship. Throughout the settler chronicles, escaped slaves are indignantly spotted fighting on the Native side, and often particularly targeted by death squads for their chutzpah.[22] Meantime, in the South, settlers enslaved both Natives and Africans, forcing their "breeding" in the captivity of the slave huts.[23] These histories resulted in the darker skin tones now seen among certain Eastern Indians, including some like the Lumbees who look downright "black" to modern racist eyes. Native lineages that did not happen to adopt Africans retained their natural "whiteness."

In the nineteenth century, as Slavery became the national hot-button issue, U.S. racism turned astoundingly dangerous—more so than it had been in the eighteenth century—yet its very ferocity caused blindness in its practitioners. Under the eye-test of racial identity introduced by, especially, Johann Friederick Blumenbach in his classic "science" of racism, *On the Natural Varieties of Mankind* (1795), alert racists were certain that they could spot racial "impurities" at a glance.[24] Ironically, their confidence in their ability to eyeball the identity of Others allowed any whose appearance did not accord with their racist fantasies to "pass." Because Blumenbach had never actually seen any of the peoples he presumed to describe, the racist norms of appearance, etched into standards surviving well into the twentieth century, actually facilitated Eastern Natives' hiding in their skin. Many Northeastern Indians were able to slide in under the racist radar, with their light skins, grey eyes, and chestnut hair.

Although the diehards were well known to exist in the East, by the late nineteenth century, Euro-American dirt farmers had adopted a live-and-let-live attitude, their lives too full of their own hardships to visit many on others. They certainly knew who the local Indian families were and countenanced their presence, so long as said Indians "kept their place," as ditch-diggers, or, like my grandmother, laundresses and basket weavers. In a fine and lucrative bit of clowning, my great-great-grandfather, Hë:töh, moved furtively about the edges of settler communities from the 1860s to 1874 as an itinerant peddler, selling tombstones to the "pioneers." This blinkered existence of

Non-Treaty Peoples in the East constituted the original Don't-Ask-Don't-Tell policy.

Ironically, one way that modern Eastern Natives can show their identity is through the *anti*-documentation that resulted from documentary genocide. Since Jacksonian Removal had declared the Eastern United States Indian-*rein*, federal census takers flatly refused to record the existence of Eastern Natives from 1845 well into the twentieth century. Native families were there, and perfectly well known as Indians to the locals; they were just not officially noticed, so that absence from the U.S. Census between Removal and the mid-twentieth century almost always means that the family was Indian. (African Americans *were* recorded.)

Under this perverted system, just being recorded somewhere conferred the indubitable advantage of allowing Natives to exercise legal and civil rights as "whites." For instance, anyone wishing to set up a farm in West Virginia had better have been "white," because it was against the law for Indians to own property in that state *until 1964*. Racial laws everywhere in America made it illegal to marry outside of one's race until the 1960s. When a Native's significant Other was African American, no one raised red flags, but, should the offending Other be "white," all sorts of KKK-enforced damage could result from the "miscegenation." In most instances, therefore, "passing for white" was the only sane option for Natives east of the Mississippi.

This logic may appear contemptible to those for whom sinking into oblivion with one's doomed cause carries a glamorous cachet. For any who have ever actually been doomed, however, willful sinking just seems immature. The main coup of Eastern holdouts back then was far less melodramatic than twinkling out of existence. It was, instead, to get their family name registered on a U.S. Census, for then, the family could claim to be "white." This was an act of reverse pen-and-ink witchcraft undertaken on theory that any Indian who wanted to lie to the settlers should do so in writing. That way, they would never catch on. Lying to the census taker was impossible when locals were retained as census agents, but, should an outsider be hired to take the Census, he might be fooled. Of course, tricksters had to be wary, for having discovered what was afoot, a spiteful census taker might record tricksters as "colored" or "mulatto," putting them in an even worse legal and civil position than they had been as invisibly Indian.[25]

Dangerous though it was, many an Eastern family holds the tradition of an ancestor who lied to the Census Man. In fact, my own great-grandmother, Wari ("Mary"), purportedly very beautiful in her youth, cleverly got herself up as a white woman to inveigle the outsider taking the 1880 Census into recording her family as "white," in an entry that is riotously funny today for its complete lunacy. She affirmed, among other things, that her father, Hë:töh, was still alive (he had died of cholera in 1874) and that her mother was from Russia. Grandma Wari chose Russia because, having fraternized with some Russian Jews, she promptly decided that all Russians were dark-haired and beak-nosed, as were many Natives.

Actually, Wari's mother, Grandma Barbara, was a Grey-Eyes, Snake Clan Wyandot, adopted into the Bear Clan of the Ohio Senecas in 1843. Born in Ontario, Canada, at sixteen, Barbara "escaped" the Catholic nuns holding her captive (her characterization) in a mission school. Stealing a canoe, she paddled along the edge of Lake Erie south, into the Miami of the Lake (the Maumee River) in search of the holdouts who she knew were hiding in the swamps, a popular refuge since 1783. There, she met and married Hë:töh. Barbara kept her mission name, because she felt she had earned it. (The French nuns called her *Barbará*, The Barbarian, because they found her so ungovernable.) Grandma Wari—who vainly knocked ten, and in later life, even *twenty*, years off her own age—also falsified everyone's ages in the census entry, while leaving one sister entirely off the roster, for some expedient reason long since forgotten. Our family never appeared on the Census before or after Wari's 1880 ruse, until name and town changes (not to mention the Termination program) in the mid-twentieth century facilitated social movement.

After Grandma Wari had counted coup on the Census Man, and to the end of her centenarian life in 1949, she sat on her front porch every evening, patiently waiting for the sheriff to come arrest her for lying to the government. She never was dragged up on charges, but her ploy backfired, by alerting social workers to her whereabouts. They duly packed her children off to the government kid prison called Indian Boarding School. Warí eventually located three but recovered only two, one of whom stalked angrily away from his heritage—although he was quite happy, in the 1960s, to demand a handsome chunk of the proceeds, when financial necessity finally forced the family to sell its old Dawes allotment.

As in Grandma Warí's deceit, the Euro-American expectation that all Indians spoke jibberish while swathing their dark skin in feathers and blankets worked *against* detection. All the diehards had to do, was go against stereotype. To live unmolested, Eastern holdouts perforce adopted Western dress, along with European languages. Wearing European clothing was hardly a new or difficult development. In another violation of racist stereotypes—this one, of the static nature of "savagery"—Eastern Natives had always been quick to update their customs. In this instance, they had been happily using woven cloth, especially flannel and wool, since contact.

Adopting English was another matter, however, a direct artifact of nineteenth- and twentieth-century survival. First, most of the Indian Boarding School staff were so poorly educated themselves, that they were barely functional in English, let alone in any other language. Consequently, English, the language of the teachers, was rammed down the children's throats. Second, government officials deliberately mixed nations and separated siblings, the better to suppress home languages. Teachers did not want siblings conversing freely behind their backs. Separating families was a trick officials had learned during the era of Slavery, as a good way to demoralize captives and keep them from the sense of community so important to acting in their own behalf.

In the Northeast, the matter was further complicated by the use of French, which was actually its important "white" tongue. French, too, was conclusively cut out during the Boarding School period by Francophobe martinets who abhorred French as avidly as they did Native languages. Although I have never seen it stated in records of the period, I strongly suspect that school officials feared that French might constitute a *lingua franca* among Indian "scholars" of unrelated nations.

Not wanting students to speak privately, and thereby evade the constant surveillance that was the Boarding School norm, teachers "civilized" the French right out of Northeastern Natives.

If Western reservation children had some hope of thwarting language loss during this dismal period, because they still heard their languages spoken during visits home, it was never safe for Northeastern peoples to speak home languages. Families in hiding Anglicized their own tongues, wrapping them around English to avoid detection. Consequently, English was successfully imposed in the Northeast. Between Boarding School and the scattered, hidden nature of diehard collectives here, it eventually became next to impossible to pass along much of the old languages. On the League reservations of New York in 1998, only twenty-five fluent speakers of Seneca remained. As of the turn of the twenty-first century, only a handful of known birth speakers of Ohio Seneca remain alive. Eastern languages are unquestionably struggling for survival; even on the scarce Eastern reservations, too few make the old talk, and fewer still listen to learn it.

Of course, loss of everday language does constitute some loss of culture, for the sorts of conceptual distinctions natural to home languages are only clumsily translated into English. For instance, in Iroquois, it is not natural to refer to human beings in terms of "color," and it is flatly impossible to use a possessive pronoun to describe another human being. People are described in terms of who arrived at a given geographical place first and the sociopolitical relationships that developed between newcomers and veterans. Thus, one cannot say, "That *black* woman is *my* sister." One must say, "That younger Salt Being and I are sisters," a far more enlightened way to look at identity and relationships than the Euro-American characterizations of "black" and "my."[26]

If simple grammar is a linguistic headache, larger conceptual points are even more of a trial to express. How does one convey that half of the cosmos is naturally Sky and Male, just as the other half is essentially Earth and Female? (West of the Mississippi, this distinction is often posited as Air and Water, respectively.) The simple gendering of Romance languages is riddle enough for most English speakers. It is next to impossible to convey in comprehensible English the pervasive, bedrock perception, built into the languages, of the Native universe as existing by complementary and interdependent halves.

Consequently, I agree with our Western cousins that language must be recovered, nor do I despair of its being possible, despite the massive damage done by cultural genocide. The sterling examples of both the Jews and the Celts are heartening here. As early as 1922, twenty-six years before the founding of the State of Israel, Hebrew was declared the official language of the Jews of Palestine, despite its having been pronounced dead a couple of millennia before. Once Jews began in-gathering in numbers in 1948 from diasporic homes as unconnected as Poland and India, Hebrew truly caught on in everyday usage. Similarly, racist British policies had driven Celtic languages into near oblivion by the mid-twentieth century, but Gaelic was heartily revived in the 1980s, and in 2005, Scotland declared Gaelic its official language, with the British Crown forced to bless the fact in legislation of its own. The same revival can be accomplished with Native languages in the East. Given the five hundred years' worth of linguistic transcriptions by Christian missionaries, the raw materials certainly exist for language recovery in the present.

Furthermore, some Eastern elders retained their languages into the early, mid-, and even late-twentieth century. Today, in the twenty-first century, some—including Thomas McElwain, a West Virginia Seneca ("Mingo"), and Grandmother Barbara Crandell, an Ohio Cherokee—yet retain their birth languages. In modern times, with visible Indian identity less immediately lethal to one's health, there is an effort to come forward and reclaim those languages through "language camps" such as have been offered in Ohio, where children are immersed in and expected solely to use, say, the Ohio Iroquoian dialect for the duration of the camp-out. There is also a "Mingo" listserv that focuses exclusively on the Ohio Iroquoian dialect, which is actually Western Seneca (Erie).

The rub with Native language revivals in the East is that very few federally recognized Indians live here. This does not mean, as is cavalierly concluded, that no Indians exist in the East; it just means that the hundreds of thousands who do, have no hope of garnering federal aid in rebuilding their languages, adding immeasurably to the burden of language preservation. As a result, people who manage Eastern language retrieval do so as individuals, entirely out of their own pockets and on their own time. Not only does the lack of federal help make operations smaller and slower than they would be if aid were available, but it also makes it difficult for seekers to find the archives, speakers, and materials. Unless the private individuals running the resuscitation efforts publicize their whereabouts (thus inviting every kook to come out of the woodwork at them), the projects remain as effectively hidden as Eastern Indians, themselves.

The suggestion I have heard, that Eastern Natives get themselves recognized, is hardly helpful. No one who has not tried to gain federal recognition—or *regain* it, once it has been yanked, for that matter—has the slightest idea of just how agonizingly difficult the federal government makes the process. Having spent the last century and a half fervently backing its documentary genocide against us, the federal government is not about to switch gears by conceding that the East is literally teeming with unRemoved, Non-Treaty Indians. Typically, as with the Pokagon Band of Indiana Potawatomis in 1994, gaining recognition requires special congressional legislation, signed by the president. The Miamis of Indiana form a more common case in point. Although these Miamis are undoubtedly who they say the are, regardless of the level of documentation they proffer, the federal government continually (and gleefully, I think) rejects their petition to enjoy the same recognition as their transported kin, off-loaded in Kansas.

This lack of federal recognition is often held against Eastern Natives by their Western cousins, but again, a sheer oblivion of history deforms perception. All too many Euro-Americans, not to mention "carded" Natives, mistakenly hallow federal enrollment as THE hallmark of authenticity, rather than revile it for what it is, the trademark of conquest. Worse, they freely dismiss any who lack federal recognition as liars, frauds, or "wannabees." Since around 1970, article upon article has rolled out from under the self-righteous pens of carded Indians, from Rayna Green to Joy Harjo, denigrating unenrolled peoples for having the audacity to claim their birthright, despite the lack of federal permission to say who they are. It was Vine Deloria Jr., himself, who first popularized the slur, "Cherokee Princess" to demean unrecognized Easterners.[27]

Such sadistic cruelty, visited on Indians by other Indians, is unconscionable. I hereby call it to account.

Federal recognition is a shell game, with status deliberately parceled out by the government to *some*, but not *all*, Indians. The cynical among us consider this a divide-and-conquer tactic, for it certainly pits an in-crowd awarded federal status against outcasts excluded from it. The catcalling that results borders on the maniacal, with almost all of the din unfortunately set up by Indians launching stink bombs at other Indians. The only upshot of the potshots is to relieve the cowboys of the necessity of killing the Indians, for the Indians are doing a bang-up job of annihilating one another, all by their lonesome. In this shameful brawl, praise belongs to those who refuse to act the part of wind-up dolls, sicced on "lesser" versions of themselves by latent colonialism.

Literally nothing could be farther from true traditionalism than the capricious ostracization that results from the federal recognition tap dance. Traditional culture sought to *include* as many people as possible. The whole point of Native adoption, one of the most ancient and widespread of Native American laws, was precisely to undercut the impulse to hostile exclusion by making the Other, the Self. The minute we all "eat from one bowl" using "one spoon," as the Northeastern metaphor goes, we are relatives, forbidden to make war upon one another.[28]

Federal recognition dumps the cultural contents out of this bowl and crushes the spoon beneath its boot heel. Instead of soft-spoken relations, respecting each other's cultures and territories, it turns Natives into zero-sum competitors, all vying for the too few slots begrudgingly made available by the government. Haughty status-hogging results, replicating one of the most craven aspects of European culture. Intent on cornering control by refusing entry to those huddled outside the federal fort, governmentally created elites erect false walls of caste and "blood." This behavior is not the measure of Indian authenticity but, I regret to say, the seal of collaboration with colonialism.

Whenever I have made bold to express this analysis to recognized cousins, I have been met with indignant horror, heavy on the invective, berating me for letting in those doggone New Agers. I realize that there are some Euro-Americans who would seize on and restructure Native culture into an exotic pull-toy for the amusement of culture tourists. Indeed, I have met more than a few of these latter-day colonials, yet more of them were historians, archaeologists, and anthropologists than New Agers. My experience here is why I know that *all* varieties of cultural interloper are spectacularly easy to spot, leaving me very little respect for those Indians who cannot tell the players without a federal score card. They cannot have been paying sufficient attention to the shell game.

The game, as initiated by the Dawes Act, was this: to seize the land bases remaining to Natives out West. The original law expected the Western "tribes"—another slur term insultingly imposed by the Supreme Court in 1901[29]—to list all of their members eligible for land allotment, thus to facilitate breaking up the land mass into small, family-owned plots of 160, 80, or 40 acres. Of course, there was much more communal land than could be allotted like this, so that the vast remainder of Indian Territory was to be sold as "surplus" to non-Natives. Obviously, the fewer eligible Indians there were, the larger the land bounty available for immediate seizure by the settlers.

Things did not go quite as planned. Governmentally installed councils of the most assimilated members of those "tribes" began selling enrollment for hefty bribes and/or retracting enrollments out of petty spite over intercine disputes (practices still alive today, alas).[30] Meantime, traditional laws integrating non-Native spouses and other adoptees into the community placed Euro- and African Americans on the rolls.[31] Even without these confusions, the rolls were horribly inaccurate, because they were based on earlier missionary rolls, which had *never* included the traditionals, who evaded christianization and enumeration at all costs.

Simple administration was hardly the only rock in the road to enrollment. So hostile were Western traditionals to enrollment and allotment of their land, that they lied to Indian agents, refused to enroll, mailed allotment deeds back to the federal government, hid each other out, and, when cornered, assumed the names of their enemies rather than be listed themselves.[32] Partly, resistance was because individual property rights (following paternal lineages) was utterly destructive of matrilineal, communal Native cultures, and partly it was because Natives realized that allotment was a scheme to separate them from their remaining land base. Indians also knew then what all too many have forgotten today, that enrollment was a *benefits determination*, in the ultimate service of cultural genocide. Once families had accepted their allotments, their members became U.S. citizens who were legally stripped of their Indian identities. Forever.

Frustrated that Natives positively refused to get with the program, Congress lumbered into action. Because minimizing the number of Indians eligible to receive land was a primary goal, a special law, 25 Stat. L, 392, was passed in 1888, declaring that Indian women who married Euro-American men were no longer Native, and neither were their children. Both women and children were categorically declared "white," with no chance of regaining their Native status. Ever. Eight years later, allotment was forced on recalcitrant lineages by the Curtis Act of 1896, whether or not deeds were accepted by the enrollees. Once deeds were issued, the Curtis Act expunged the receiving families' names from the rolls. Forever. Between these two acts, untold hundreds of thousands of Natives were officially denied recognition. Francis E. Leupp, the commissioner of the Bureau of Indian Affairs in 1905, knew he was engineering cultural genocide with these exclusions, cheerfully terming his plan "the final solution" to the government's Indian problem.[33]

The Dawes Commission was also formed on June 10, 1896, by 29 Stat. L, 321, to finalize the rolls and allotments, the better to get on with land seizure. It set up new rolls, based on the earlier rolls that it had conclusively documented as corrupt. The Dawes Commission then flew by the seat of its soiled pants, making up rules as it went along and flagrantly violating those same rules whenever it felt convenient. Ever mindful of the need to authorize as few allotments as possible, the Commission summarily rejected 200,000 of those 300,000–odd Indians who defied their traditional elders to seek Dawes enrollment. When rejected applicants protested to the courts that they were unquestionably Indian and had applied according to the Dawes guidelines, the courts curtly reminded them that being Indian *was not the criterion for enrollment.*[34]

Even as it ruled known Indians off the rolls, the Commission allowed (for bribes) the enrollment of African Americans with no lineal descent or community-recognized ties.[35] One hundred and sixty acres in Oklahoma beat forty acres and a mule in Mississippi four times over, and settlers afflably viewed African enrollments as way station along the road to land transfer. (Stealing land from Freedmen was almost as easy as stealing it from Natives.) Worse, the Commission, which was also known to take corporate kickbacks, countenanced the enrollment of Euro-American employees of, for instance, logging companies. These enrollees promptly sold "their" allotments to their employers for a tidy bonus.[36] Today, Euro-Americans doing genealogical research sometimes come across an ancestor's name on a Dawes Roll and, instead of realizing that aforementioned ancestor was a crook, assume he was an Indian. Personally, I find this hilarious and, also, radicalizing. Thinking they are Native has opened the eyes of many a descendant of horse thieves to the histories and struggles of Native America.

When contested, the Dawes system was upheld in federal courts. Many challenges came from Eastern Indians, who found that the settlers were not about to get up off any of the acreage already seized in the East just to grant this or that diehard 160 acres of it. Only a minuscule number of "absentee allotments" were granted east of the Mississippi River, so that the only alternative for Eastern Natives was to out themselves racially, apply for Western land, and brace for a visit from the Ku Klux Klan. The government was even less thrilled by this prospect than the self-outers, for alloting Western land to Eastern Indians just resulted in more prime real estate "lost" to the settlers.

The federal courts fixed this pesky problem by legally barring Eastern Indians from enrolling. No one who was not physically located in Indian Territory was allowed even to apply for federal status.[37] To comply with this obstructionist rule, some Eastern Natives took the massive step—a step they had fought, tooth and nail, for half a century—of abandoning the graves of their ancestors, only to be blocked from enrollment once they arrived in Indian Territory by the self-same courts that had created the geographical mandate in the first place.[38] Under this catch-22, unless an Eastern person had prior rights on one of the scarce Eastern reservations, there was no hope of enrollment. A very few Eastern groups, including the North Carolina Cherokees and the Mississippi Choctaws, doggedly pursued enrollment in situ, but the vast majority were denied their identity by Dawes. Forever.

I often urge my students to consider what these arbitrary policies meant to the people on the ground, excluded by fiat from their identities. I ask whether there are any Christians in the room, and when hands shoot up, I ask them what would happen if the government set up federal Christian enrollment but capriciously allowed only one-third of them to register as Christian. Would the other two-thirds cease to be Christian? What if, I ask, the favored third began sneering at the rejected applicants, telling them that they had lost their faith or had never been Christians in the first place? Once my students realize how stunningly hurtful *that* would be, I ask them to consider how they, among the excluded two-thirds, would feel, should a non-Christian be allowed to enroll as Christian to receive chunks of their land, land they were federally barred from claiming. It is quickly apparent to them that although Dawes enrollment might have been legal, it was immoral and unethical. In pursuit of land seizure, it neither conferred nor demolished Indian identity.

The Dawes Commission had yet other tricks up its dingy sleeve, these hinging on a hot new pseudoscience of race that was just then all the rage. Jealous of the acclaim lavished on Charles Darwin—a cousin whom his family had always regarded as dimwitted—Francis Galton pouted up a new "science" of his own, which he pompously named "eugenics" (meaning "well born").[39] Eugenics took survival of the fittest and, based on class and race, ratcheted it up to a dead-bang determinant of human worth, with the elimination of "undesirables" a centerpiece of "hygienic" population control. Engineering for a brighter future, social darwinists—the same, fun folks who brought us the Jewish Holocaust—warmed up by imposing Nuremburgian-like laws on Native America in the form of Galtonian quantum counting.

Although sounding "scientific," because of Galton's math-mouthed fractions (1/2, 1/4, 1/8, 1/16, etc.), quantum counting actually derives from colonial Slavery, under which privileged slaves were classified according to the level of European admixture in their "blood." A mulatto was "half white;" a quadroon, three-quarters "white;" an octoroon, seven-eighths "white," and so on down to thirty-one parts (of thirty-two possible parts) "white." In all but name, eugenic quantums were identical to the old planter counts, right down to the refusal to recognize African-Native mixtures in "roon" land, spitting out, instead, sloppy slur terms for "Black Indians," such as "griffe," "lobo," "zambo," or my personal favorite, "piebald Negro."[40]

Although the original Dawes Act never mentioned quantum counting, in the fever of the eugenics movement, the Dawes Commission just began assigning quantums based on the Galtonian numerology of heritage. By the time the McCumber Amendments were passed in 1906, finalizing the rolls as complete and true, there was simply no question that, not only were quantums an absolute necessity, but also that the quantums recorded by the Commission were accurate.

Leaving aside for the moment the dehumanizing effect of carding people on their racial ancestry, the quantums assigned by the Dawes Commissioners were entirely fictitious, dreamed up on the spot by "white" authorities.[41] Because lower quantums of Native "blood" carried privileges in law and custom, favored collaborators were easily assigned "low" eighth and sixteenth quantums. Conversely, recalcitrant Indians, regardless of parentage, were assigned "full-blood" status, which neatly prevented them from appearing in court to testify against the settlers. Thus, the Dawes Commission piled delusional heritage atop utterly corrupted rolls, in the unappealable language of eugenic "science."

Today, that the United States continues using Dawes-era eugenics in carding Indians is mind-boggling. Worse, it is *popular*. It seems to give many Euro-Americans a happy, tingly feeling. People who would never dream of asking Condoleezza Rice to state her Negro Quantums (derived from the 1907 Jim Crow Commission Rolls), and who would certainly be clocked if they required David Horowitz to provide his family Reich Citizenship papers (courtesy of the Nuremburg Commission of 1935), have not the slightest hesitation about demanding "Indian papers" from Natives. Once, I even had an editor tell me that she *had* to ask me my quantums before she could publish a piece of mine. I replied that she *had* to do no such thing, that enforcing racism was a *choice* she was making all on her own, a reply that pretty much cut off any further communication.

Every time otherwise rational and unbiased people quiz me about my "quantums," I wonder whether they realize the genocidal depths of the racism into which they have just descended. If I ask as much, my interlocutors become defensive, curtly informing me that my parents contributed halves; my grandparents, quarters; and my great-grandparents, eighths of my being. This riposte does not allay, but only intensifies, my astonishment, because it accepts without cavil the major tenet of full-blown eugenics: that mentality and culture are biologically transmitted.

For the record, all races are intellectually equal, and culture is learned. A good preparation can fit anyone for the Ivy League, just as lack of it will consign her to community college. Culturally, a Chinese baby adopted and raised by Sunni Muslims will grow up to be a Sunni Muslim. A Native American infant adopted and raised by Anglo-Baptists will grow up to be an Anglo-Baptist. People imbibe whatever culture they are exposed to by their primary caregivers. This is THE reason that the Geneva Convention on Genocide outlaws as cultural genocide the transferral of children from one ethnic group to another. It is likewise the reason that modern Native and African Americans have forced child welfare agencies to stop placing their children with Euro-American families. They know that such children will grow up bereft of their heritages.

No, it is not by "full blood" that people acquire their identity; it is by living in, with, and through their culture. I have met plenty of enrolled Indians who know next to nothing about their home cultures—or, worse, purvey the missionary-mangled version of their cultures—just as I personally know an abundance of unenrolled Indians who know a great deal about their traditions. To the extent that modern Eastern Natives retain their old ways of knowing and the knowledge gained thereby, they retain every right to their Native identities.

Understanding the slimy, racist, and partial provenance of enrollment, I have often laughed at the way that some government-issue Indians wave their quantum cards aloft, as their proof of legitimacy. Since enrollment is just a benefits determination, I have often wondered what would happen should welfare recipients start waving around *their* cards to prove that they, and they alone, were the true poor people of this country. If the working poor surfaced, they could be derided as "wannabees" for their lack of federal recognition. The enrolled poor could then walk tall, as the *real* poor people of America. By flashing their cards at, say, journalists and public officials, they could gain respect as the only accredited experts on poor culture.

Yes, yes, I know that the money supporting Indian programs theoretically comes from trust funds endowed by the proceeds of land "sales," but the fact is that those trusts were looted, and their proceeds embezzled, by governmental officials and their friends as much as a century ago. The accounts have never been reconciled; the losses have just been shuffled and disguised.[42] The money for Indian programs comes out of current cash, exactly as welfare money does. The Congress knows, the public knows, and most Indians, whether or not they will admit it, know that enrollment cards are welfare cards. By contrast, Non-Treaty Eastern Indians are quite proud of the fact that they have been successfully self-supporting for a century and a half.

After decades of thought, and an excruciating amount of research, I have concluded that:

1. Eastern holdouts were justified in refusing treaties, despite the rights fights that have followed; and
2. Our problems of land and identity all grow from the same root: The wrong gender has been running the show.

Regarding the first, their very lack of recognition means that Non-Treaty Peoples can climb off the gerbil wheel of treaty rights to come at cultural survival from other than federally invented directions. Take the issue of land. All of Ohio was illegally seized. So what? Non-Treaty Indians know that, but they also know that they have no hope at law of retrieving land by challenging the treaties. Even if, by some unexampled miracle, Non-Treaty People won a case, the recovered land would be given to the enrolled people out West not to the locals who put up the fight to reclaim it. Instead of kicking against the colonial wall built by federal treaties and recognition, Eastern Natives are free to use their hard-won knowledge of European-style economics to *buy* back ancestral lands. Especially as the national economy tanks in culturally rich homelands like Ohio, the land becomes affordable.

Regarding the second, I look at the fine fix Native America is in and realize that this is exactly why the old Clan Mothers refused to let the men discuss anything that the women had not first canvassed thoroughly. In fact, the women even gave the men the preferred possible outcomes of debate, restricting them to discussions of that preset agenda.[43] Looking about today, I attribute the nightmarish morass of federal laws and "tribal" policies to the fact that they are male constructs of female issues. This upside-down situation will not be righted until women resume taking care of their Mother, which simply will not happen under Euro-American law.

Traditionally speaking, in the East, Our Mother, the Earth, is emphatically female. Among the Iroquois, for instance, Mother Earth is the Daughter of Sky Woman, for whom the female Turtle Island (North America) was made in the first place. The female descendants of that First Daughter continue to "own" the land, even as her male desdendants "own" the Sky.[44] It is recorded in the Iroquois Constitution that "Women shall be considered the progenitors of the Nation. They shall own the land and the soil."[45] Furthermore, the women, alone, control identity among both born and adopted citizens.[46] These same laws are followed by all Eastern nations. Consequently, in the East, anyhow, Native *women* are the sole, appropriate arbiters of land and identity, for it is women's feet that always remain planted firmly on Mother Earth, whereas men's fly up to Brother Sky.

When men attempt to manage Earth matters, like land and identity, they confuse themselves by applying Sky principles of height and distance. The outcome is as predictable as it is disastrous: Flighty rules result from their eagle's-eye view, obviating ground matters, which look too small to make out from the vantage point of Sky. Unable to feel the rumblings of *ne gashedenza* (the sacred will of the people), which traditionally originates at the roots of the grass, they grab for the wind and blow hot air.

Women are the ones who feel the vibrations of the growing grass, through the soles of their feet and the waters of their wombs. They are the ones who know their descendants, arrayed by clan, through the generations. It is the women who keep the names and pull the ancestors out of the ground, back into life, even as they pull the crops up from seeds. It is the women who can tell the ordinary dirt from the dirt made of their ancestors, the first five feet down. They can sense the land, for the land is a woman. It is, therefore, the Daughters of Mother Earth who make the best decisions regarding the children and the land of Mother Earth.

It is in validation of this truth that it is, today, the women of the East who are rescuing their Mother from the less-than-gentle stewardship of male Euro-Americans, who now find her worthless, having sucked her teats dry of their nutrients, pumped her bowels clean of their oils, pulled the digestive coals free from her gizzards, and razed the landscape of her lungs, the trees. Purchasing back the land, Eastern women lovingly forbid the fertilizers, which have weakened their Mother's bones. Instead, they encourage new lungs to emerge, as they scatter water prayers for recovery over her prone and wretched body. Now, the women's feet can touch, again, the dirt skin of their Mother, and Her spirits of place can once more flow up from the ground to inform the people of who they are and where they belong.

Consequently, women must reclaim custody of identity. The hysteria surrounding the recognition game results directly from the overweening power so wrongly granted males, including adolescent males, in the matter. Everywhere in the world that men rule to the exclusion of women, the result is havoc, and the younger the men, the speedier the course to bedlam. I have often pondered what might happen in the so-called Middle East should the men be forced to step aside, as they were in the Eastern woodlands, so that the Grandmothers, those only proper guardians of peace and war, might address one another without the clamor of Sky-spinning males demanding everyone's attention. The direct result in the Northeastern woodlands was that male-dominated governments and the wars they promoted were outlawed, from the twelfth century forward, as the old, priest-run mound cultures were dismantled.[47]

Thereafter, it was women, alone, who appointed soldiers and who called—and called off—the wars.[48] When rival sides arose, the Grandmothers quelled hostilities by reasoning together, saying, "Let us look at our children and remember that we did not bring these younger ones into the world, lavish loving care upon them their whole lives, and make them into these magnificent youths, just to watch them die hasty and foolish deaths. No, no: it is far wiser to feed all from the same bowl, exchange gifts, and teach the rising generations the songs of their ancestors."[49] When women's speakers appeared in plenary councils, they always began by reminding the men of the prime law of the woodlands: the absolute right of women and children to peace and security.[50]

The same, traditional rule by Grandmother needs to be observed in the matter of identity. By *all* the laws of the East, the Councils of Grandmothers, alone, determine who is who, and, moreover, they determine it exclusively through the female line. Far from the noisome and largely imaginary busy-ness of quantum-counting, the Grandmothers know their communities and their descendants. They know that anyone born of a Indian mother is *100 percent Indian*, whereas no one born of a Native father is Native unless formally adopted by the Grandmothers. This means that the vaunted quantums of the federal government, shoved through the unlikely birth canal of the father, are fictive. To become accepted as an Indian, the child of a Native father and non-Native mother must apply to the Grandmothers for adoption.

The point at which the Grandmothers see fit to adopt such a person is the point at which that person becomes *fully* Indian.

Obviously, this system flies in the face of federal mischief, as in the case of Gawaso Wanneh (Arthur Caswell Parker, 1855–1955), the famed Seneca anthropologist. Western racists (and just about everyone Euro-American he worked with was a racist) never hesitated in the slightest to finger Gawaso Wanneh as "one-eighth Indian"—or to denigrate him and his work as a direct result of his race. Nevertheless, since his "blood" came through the male line, the Senecas did not consider him Seneca at all until the Grandmothers of the Bear Clan formally adopted him, after which he was considered completely Seneca.[51] Notice that *adoption*—not rejection or sadistic name-calling—is the traditional response of Grandmothers to questions of identity.[52]

In a resurrection of Indian ways of dealing with Indian issues, I propose that elder women, treaty and Non-Treaty alike, come together in a nationwide council to strengthen Indian bonds, East and West. This council will be run the old way, by the Grandmothers, their feet firmly rooted to the ground, judging other women by their messages and their deeds. Each woman is to bring the best gift of her community, to share unstintingly with all her relatives. All points will be patiently heard, and in the voices that raise them. Only once they have thoroughly examined the issues and concluded likely answers will the women turn the matter over to the men, retaining the right to overrule them, should their feet fly too far off the ground.

There is much that stands to be salvaged and revitalized once the Daughters of Mother Earth establish this new gifting alliance. The gift brought by Western Indians, that of experience with language trusts, will be very helpful in the East, while the gift brought by Eastern Indians, that of retaining non-christianized traditions, will prove quite helpful in the West. The Western knowledge of how to navigate around federal shoals without being sucked under by governmental riptides will complement Eastern knowledge of how to walk in two worlds without being torn apart psychically. Then, the people can sit together on the ground in the old way, taking turns to tell one another their traditions, each speaker being met with respect, acceptance, and lively attention.

So be it.

NOTES

1. *Hanötaká:nyas* literally translates as "He Consumes It by Fire" or "He Burns It." In Native discourse in the Eastern woodlands, singular pronouns stand for entire groups. In this instance, "He" is the American Army, although George Washington, who ordered the genocide, was and is frequently referred to personally as "The Town Burner." In 1926, Arthur Parker, a Seneca and a scholar, rendered *Hanötaká:nyas* as "The Hollocaust" [*sic*], in Arthur C[aswell] Parker, [*Gawaso Waneh*], *An Analytical History of the Seneca Indians*, Researches and Transactions of the New York State Archaeological Association, Lewis H. Morgan Chapter (1926, reprint; New York: Kraus Reprint, 1970), p. 126.

2. Ian K Steele, *Warpaths: Invasions of North America* (New York: Oxford University Press, 1994), p. 142.

3. For the story of the Goschocking genocide, see Barbara Alice Mann, *George Washington's War on Native America* (Westport, CT: Praeger, 2005), pp. 147–69.

4. For a typical visitor repudiation, see one example in Arthur Caswell Parker, "The Maize Maiden," in *Rumbling Wings and Other Indian Tales* (Garden City, NY: Doubleday, Doran and Company, 1928), p. 186.

5. Board of Indian Commissioners, *Annual Report*, 1885, *House Executive Documents*, 49th Congress, Session I, no. 109 (Washington, DC: Government Printing Office, 1901), pp. 90–91.

6. *The Eastern Band of Cherokees v. The United States and the Cherokee Nation*, 20 Ct. Cl. 449, 479 (1885), in *Cases Decided in the Court of Claims at the Term of 1884–'85*, vol. 20 (Washington, DC: Government Printing Office, 1885), pp. 449–83, quotes on p. 479 and p. 480, respectively.

7. *Eastern Band of Cherokee Indians v. United States and Cherokee Nation, Commonly Called Cherokee Nation West,* 117 U.S. 288 (1885), in *United States Reports,* vol. 117, *Cases Adjudged in The Supreme Court at October Term 1885* (New York: Banks and Brothers, Law Publishers, 1886), pp. 288–313; quote on p. 309.

8. Department of the Interior, *Annual Report of the Commissioner of Indian Affairs for the Fiscal Year Ended June 30, 1898* (Washington, DC: Government Printing Office, 1898), p. 485.

9. [Alexander McKee], *Minutes of Debates in Council on the Banks of the Ottawa River, (Commonly Called the Miami of the Lake), November, 1791* (Philadelphia: William Young, Bookseller, 1792), p. 11.

10. The term *documentary genocide* was coined by Russell Booker, a Virginia State registrar. See J. David Smith, *The Eugenic Assault on America: Scenes in Red, White, and Black* (Fairfax, VA: George Mason University Press, 1993) coining of the term, p. 111; expansion on concept, pp. 89, 100.

11. For discussions of the Black Drink, see John Heckewelder, *History, Manners, and Customs of the Indian Nations Who Once Inhabited Pennsylvania and the Neighboring States,* First American Frontier Series (1820; 1826, reprint; New York: Arno Press and the *New York Times,* 1971), p. 245; Gregory Evans Dowd, *A Spirited Resistance: North American Indian Struggle for Unity, 1745–1815* (Baltimore: Johns Hopkins University Press, 1992), pp. 33, 39, and 40. Dowd mistakenly claimed that the Shawnee had brought the Black Drink north in the eighteenth century, but John Heckewelder was clear that it was already in long usage before that time. The Lenapes brought it into the Iroquois League along with themselves in 1661.

12. Barbara Alice Mann, "'A Man of Misery': Chitto Harjo and the Senate Select Committee on Oklahoma Statehood," in Barbara Alice Mann (ed.), *Native American Speakers of the Eastern Woodlands: Selected Speeches and Critical Analyses* (Westport, CT: Greenwood, 2001), pp. 198, 215, and 223 (n. 11).

13. For a long look at the force and fraudulence of the Greenville Treaty, see Barbara Alice Mann, "The Greenville Treaty of 1795: Pen-and-Ink Witchcraft in the Struggle for the Old Northwest," in Bruce E.

Johansen (ed.), *Enduring Legacies: Native American Treaties and Contemporary Controversies* (Westport, CT: Praeger, 2004), pp. 135–201.

14. In 1783, Benjamin Franklin recorded much the same complaint about Natives who had been taken by the missionaries for "christianization," except that, in translation, the phrase came out "bad Runners" who, post-christianization, were "totally good for nothing." Benjamin Franklin, *Writings* (New York: Library of America, 1987), p. 970.

15. Francis Paul Prucha, *The Great Father: The United States Government and the American Indians*, 2 vols. (Lincoln: University of Nebraska Press, 1984): 1: pp. 349–50.

16. See, for instance, see Adriaen Cornelissen van der Donck, "Description of New Netherland," 1653; trans. Diederick Goedhuys, in Dean Snow, Charles T. Gehring, and William A. Starna (eds.), *In Mohawk Country: Early Narrative about a Native People* (Syracuse: Syracuse University Press, 1996), pp. 106, 107; Benjamin Smith Barton, *New Views of the Origin of the Tribes and Nations of America* (1798, reprint; Millwood, NY: Kraus Reprint, 1976), p. xlv; Gabriel Sagard, *The Long Journey to the Country of the Hurons*, ed. George M. Wrong, trans. H. H. Langton (1632; Toronto: Champlain Society, 1939), p. 136; Rueben Gold Thwaites (ed. and trans.), *The Jesuit Relations: Travels and Explorations of the Jesuit Missionaries in New France, 1610–1791*, 73 vols. (New York: Pageant Book Company, 1959) 5: p. 23; Samuel de Champlain, *The Works of Samuel de Champlain*, ed. H. P. Biggar, trans. W. D. LeSuer and H. H. Langton, 6 vols. (Toronto: Champlain Society, 1936) 4: p. 53; Pierre de Charlevois, *Journal of a Voyage to North America*, 2 vols. (1761; Ann Arbor, MI: University Microfilms, 1966) 2: p. 90; Joseph François Lafitau, *Customs of the American Indians Compared with the Customs of Primitive Times*, ed. and trans. William N. Fenton and Elizabeth L. Moore, vol. 1 (Toronto: Champlain Society, 1974), p. 89.

17. The shipwrecked sailor theory was first suggested by Father Eusebio Kino, a Spanish conquistador roaming the old Southwest and recording tales of blonds in every which direction. See the various accounts in Herbert Eugene Bolton, *The Rim of Christendom: A Biography of Eusebio Francisco Kino, Pacific Coast Pioneer* (New York: Russell and Russell, 1960), pp. 374, 418–19. Although obviously a speculation old

enough to have whiskers, shipwrecked Europeans getting into the mix was later set down later as irrefutable fact by Justin Winsor in volume 3 of his *Narrative and Critical History of America* (1884–89): "The phenomenon of auburn and chestnut-colored hair may be [*sic*] accounted for the fact, related by the natives, that some years before a ship, manned by whites, had been wrecked on the coast; and that some of the people had been saved, and had lived with them for several weeks before leaving in their boats, in which, however, they were lost. It was the descendants of these men, *doubtless*, who were found by the English having hair unlike the other Indians." (emphasis added). Quoted in Henry S. Burrage (ed.), *Early English and French Voyages, 1534–1608: Original Narratives of Early American History* (1906; New York: Barnes and Noble, 1967), p. 233 (n. 1).

18. The Atlantean theory was quite popular and in higher places than modern scholars like to admit because it allowed "white" people to have the credit for the "high" Mound Builder cultures of North America. The most famous, though hardly the only, articulation of this nonsense was in Ignatius Donnelly, *Atlantis: The Antediluvian World*, ed. Egerton Sykes (1881; New York: Harper and Brothers, 1949). Based on Donnelly's book, Prime Minister William Edward Gladstone asked the British government to mount an expedition to find Atlantis in the Atlantic Ocean. (Donnelly, *Atlantis*, p. x). The Atlantean theory was also the basis of Joseph Smith's *Book of Mormon*, largely plagiarized from earlier clerical authors. Fawn McKay Brodie, *No Man Knows My History: The Life of Joseph Smith, The Mormon Prophet*, 2nd ed. (1945; New York: Knopf, 1971), pp. 35–43; Robert Silverberg, *Mound Builders of Ancient America: The Archaeology of a Myth* (Greenwich, CT: New York Graphic Society, 1968), pp. 94–96; original documents plagiarized: Ethan Smith, *View of the Hebrews; Exhibiting the Destruction of Jerusalem; the Certain Restoration of Judah and Israel; the Present State of Judah and Israel; and an Address of the Prophet Isaiahy Relative to their Restoration* (Poultney, VT: Smith and Shurte, 1823); and Solomon Spaulding, *The "Manuscript Found" or "Manuscript Story," of the Late Rev. Solomon Spaulding from a Verbatim Copy of the Original Now in the Care of Pres. James H. Fiarchild of Oberlin College, Ohio* (Lamoni, IA:

Reorganized Church, 1885). See also my discussion of the Atlantean theory as archaeology in Barbara Alice Mann, *Native Americans, Archaeologists, and the Mounds* (New York: Peter Lang, 2003), pp. 73–76.

19. Noah Webster, "Antiquity: Letter III. From Mr. N. Webster, to the Rev. Dr. Stiles, President of Yale College, on the Remains of the Fortifications in the Western Country. Dated New-York January 20, 1788," *American Magazine* (February 1788): pp. 146–56, esp. p. 155; and John Filson, *The Discovery and Settlement of Kentucke* (1784, reprint; Ann Arbor, MI: University Microfilms, 1966), p. 95. No one source was responsible for this craze. For a thorough discussion of the Welsh invasion craze, see Mann, *Native Americans, Archaeologists, and the Mounds*, pp. 76–81.

20. Sagard, *The Long Journey*, p. 136; Charlevoix, *Journal of a Voyage to North America*, vol. 2, p. 90.

21. Father LeJeune in his 1633–34 report in Thwaites, *Jesuit Relations*, 5: p. 23.

22. See, for instance, the contemptuous accounts of the African captured by Sullivan's forces during his genocidal sweep through Iroquoia in 1779 in Frederick Cook, *Journals of a Military Expedition of Major General John Sullivan against the Six Nations of Indians in 1779* (1887, reprint; Freeport, NY: Books for Libraries, 1972), pp. 44, 172; Albert Hazen Wright, *The Sullivan Expedition of 1779: Contemporary Newspaper Comment*, Studies in History, nos. 5, 6, 7, and 8, part 3 (Ithaca, NY: A. H. Wright, 1943), pp. 1, 3; Nathan Davis, "History of the Expedition against the Five Nations, Commanded by General Sullivan, in 1779," *Historical Magazine* 3, no. 4 (1868): p. 200. See also the deliberate targeting of the adopted African, who became the medicine man of a town in Onondaga in 1779, in Cook, *Journals*, p. 17, and the African adoptee of the Shawnees who helped her town defeat a militia raid, also in 1779, in "Bowman's Campaign of 1779," *Ohio Archaeological and Historical Publications* 22 (1913): pp. 507, 516–17; and "Bowman's Expedition against Chillicothe, May-June, 1779," *Ohio Archaeological and Historical Publications* 19 (1910): p. 457.

23. On African-Native slaves, see Jack D. Forbes, *Africans and Native Americans: The Language of Race and the Evolution of Red-Black Peoples* (Urbana: University of Illinois Press, 1993).

24. Johann Friederich Blumenbach, *On the Natural Varieties of Mankind* (1795; 1865, reprint; New York: Bergman Publishers, 1969).

25. The "mulattoization" of Natives is documented to have occurred widely. See J. David Smith's careful reconstruction of the problem in *Eugenic Assault on America*, pp. 59, 71–82, 90, 98.

26. The Mahican Aupaumut laid out this traditional system in detail in 1791, discussing Ohio councils in Hendrick Aupaumut, "A Narrative of an Embassy to the Western Indians," *Memoirs of the Historical Society of Pennsulvania*, 2, no. 1 (1827): pp. 76–77. Salt Beings are people from across the Great Salt Lake, or Atlantic Ocean. Both Europeans and Africans are younger siblings, with the Europeans the elder of the two because they were more recently seen in the Northeast than Africans. Thus, Europeans are traditionally called "younger siblings," making Africans the "youngest siblings."

27. Rayna Green, "A Tribe Called Wannabee: Playing Indian in America and Europe," *Folklore* 9, no. 1 (1988): pp. 30–55; Joy Harjo, "Identity: Part Deux," *Indian Country Today*, April 7, 2005; accessed 9 June 9, 2005, at www.indiancountry.com/content.cfm?id=1096410704; Vine Deloria Jr., *Custer Died for Your Sins: An Indian Manifesto* (1969, reprint; Norman: University of Oklahoma Press, 1988), pp. 2–4.

28. Eating from one bowl, using the same spoon is the traditional metaphor in the East for recognizing one another as relatives. See, for instance, John Heckewelder, *History, Manners, and Customs of the Indian Nations Who Once Inhabited Pennsylvania and the Neighboring States*, First American Frontier Series (1820; 1876, reprint; New York: Arno Press and *The New York Times*, 1971), pp. 269–70 (n. 1); as quoted in Richard White, *The Middle Ground: Indians, Empires, and Republics, in the Great Lakes Region, 1650–1815* (New York: Cambridge University Press, 1991), pp. 462, 469, 480–83, 512, 515.

29. "Tribe" was imposed by the *Montoya v. United States* decision, 180 U.S., 261 (1901); 21 S. Ct., 358, 359 (190) in National Reporter System, *The Supreme Court Reporter, November, 1900–July, 1901*, vol. 21 (St. Paul, MN: West Publishing, 1901), p. 35.

30. Kent Carter, "Deciding Who Can Be Cherokee: Enrollment Records of the Dawes Commission," *Chronicles of Oklahoma* 69, no. 2

(1991): p. 179. For fun and games with enrollment in modern times, see Bruce E. Johansen, "The New York Oneidas: A Business Called a Nation," in Bruce E. Johansen (ed.), *Enduring Legacies: Native American Treaties and Contemporary Controversies* (Westport, CT: Praeger, 2004), pp. 95–133.

31. Forbes, *Africans and Native Americans*, 89; Angie Debo, *And Still the Water Runs: The Betrayal of the Five Civilized Tribes* (1940; Princeton, NJ: Princeton University Press, 1991), p. 11.

32. See my discussion of this aspect of nonenrollment in Barbara Alice Mann, "'A Man of Misery': Chitto Harjo and the Senate Select Committee on Oklahoma Statehood," in Barbara Alice Mann (ed.), *Native American Speakers of the Eastern Woodlands: Selected Speeches and Critical Analyses* (Westport, CT: Greenwood, 2001), pp. 197–216.

33. Department of the Interior, *Annual Report of the Commissioner of Indian Affairs for the Fiscal Year Ended June 30, 1905*, Part 1 (Washington, DC: Government Printing Office, 1906), p. 5.

34. Department of the Interior, *Annual Report of the Commissioner of Indian Affairs for the Fiscal Year Ended June 30, 1898* (Washington, DC: Government Printing Office, 1899), p. 513.

35. Debo, *And Still the Waters Run*, pp. 42, 45, 47, 269–70; for raw Freedemen enrollment statistics, see Department of the Interior, *Annual Report of the Commissioner of Indian Affairs for the Fiscal Year Ended June 30, 1905*, Part 1, pp. 597, 600, 609, 623. See also my discussions in Mann, *Native American Speakers of the Eastern Woodlands*, pp. 210–13; and Mann, *Native Americans, Archaeologists, and the Mounds*, pp. 286–87.

36. Department of the Interior, *Annual Report to the Commissioner of Indian Affairs for 1895*, 5 vols. (Washington, DC: Government Printing Office, 1896): 2: p. 21.

37. Department of the Interior, *Annual Report of the Commissioner of Indians Affairs for the Fiscal Year Ended June 30, 1898*, pp. 500, 503, 504–5.

38. See, for instance, the cases of the Malachai Watts and Ann Crews families, as documented in Mann, *Native Americans, Archaeologists, and the Mounds*, pp. 293–94.

39. Francis Galton, *English Men of Science: Their Nature and Nurture* (New York: D. Appleton, 1875); *Hereditary Genius: An Inquiry into Its*

Laws and Consequences (1869; New York: D. Appleton, 1884); *Inquiries into Human Faculty and Its Development* (1883; London: J. M. Den, 1907); *Natural Inheritance* (1889, reprint; New York: AMS Press, 1973).

40. Blumenbach, *On the Natural Varieties of Mankind*, pp. 216–218; J. Leitch Wright, *The Only Land They Knew: The Tragic Story of the American Indians in the Old South* (New York: Free Press, 1981), p. 252; Richard Drinnon, *Facing West: The Metaphysics of Indian-Hating and Empire-Building* (Minneapolis: University of Minnesota Press, 1980), p. 107.

41. See examples of the assignment process in Kent Carter, "Deciding Who Can Be Cherokee: Enrollment Records of the Dawes Commission," *Chronicles of Oklahoma* 69, no. 2 (1991): pp. 174–205; and "Federal Indian Policy: Cherokee Enrollment, 1898–1907," *Prologue* 23, no. 1 (1991): pp. 25–31.

42. Government Accounting Office, "The BIA's Tribal Trust Fund Account Reconciliation Results," Report number GAO/AIMD–96–93, Report to the Committee on Indian Affairs, U.S. Senate, May 3, 1996.

43. Charlevoix, *Journal of a Voyage*, 2: 26; Lafitau, *Customs of the American Indians*, 2: p. 295; Lucien Carr, "On the Social and Political Position of Woman among the Huron-Iroquois Tribes," Peabody Museum of American Archaeology and Ethnology, Reports 16 and 17, no. 3.3–4 (1884): p. 55; Renee Jacobs, "Iroquois Great Law of Peace and the United States Constitution: How the Founding Fathers Ignored the Clan Mothers," Notes, *American Indian Law Review* 16, no. 2 (1991): p. 503.

44. Barbara A. Mann, "Haudenosaunee (Iroquois) Women, Legal and Political Status," in Bruce Elliott Johansen (ed.), *The Encyclopedia of Native American Legal Tradition* (Westport, CT: Greenwood, 1998), pp. 112–31.

45. Arthur C. Parker, *The Constitution of the Five Nations, or the Iroquois Book of the Great Law* (Albany: University of the State of New York, 1916), p. 42.

46. Parker, *Constitution*, pp. 42–44.

47. The Iroquois Constitution, which conferred extraordinary powers on women socially, economically, and politically, was ratified

in 1142 following the major civil war that forced the old priest-run culture of the Mound Builders into well-deserved oblivion. For the founding of the League, see Barbara A. Mann and Jerry L. Fields, "A Sign in the Sky: Dating the League of the Haudenosaunee," *American Indian Culture and Research Journal* 21, no. 2 (1997): pp. 105–63. For Eastern mound culture and its demise, see Mann, *Native Americans, Archaeologists, and the Mounds*, pp. 155–68. For the extraordinary powers of Eastern women, see Barbara Alice Mann, *Iroquoian Women: The Gantowisas* (New York: Lang, 2004).

48. Steve Wall, *Wisdom's Daughters: Conversations with Women Elders of Native America* (New York: Harper Perennial, 1993), p. 253; Lafitau, *Customs of the American Indians*, 2: p. 99; Charlevoix, *Journal of a Voyage to North America*, vol. 1, p. 317; Carr, "On the Social Position of Woman," pp. 223–24.

49. See the example of just such a speech delivered by the Iroquoian Grandmothers to the Lenape Grandmothers when the latter nation was taken in under the protective shade of the Tree of Peace, that is, incorporated into the Iroquois League in 1661, in Heckewelder, *History, Manners, and Customs*, p. 57.

50. See, for instance, the Women's Speaker, Ab, beth, din, Wyrosh, Yeshivo, on this subject, in McKee, *Minutes of Debates*, pp. 20–21.

51. For adoption, see William N. Fenton, "Introduction," *Parker on the Iroquois* (New York: Syracuse University Press, 1968), p. 13; for examples of denigration on grounds of race, see Fenton, "Introduction," pp. 6, 7, 8, 10, 28. For my earlier discussion on this issue, see Barbara Alice Mann, "Euro-Forming the Data," in Bruce E. Johansen (ed.), *Debating Democracy: Native American Legacy of Freedom* (Santa Fe: Clear Light, 1998), pp. 178–80.

52. Typically, there are three levels of adoption: the lineage level, the clan level, and the national level. In the first instance, the Grandmothers of a particular female lineage publicly embrace a new member, usually at a Green Corn or Midwinter festival, just after all the new babies born that year are introduced to the assembled relatives. In the second event, the Grandmothers of all the lineages within a given clan decide by consensus that such-and-such an adoptee has proven herself

to the point that she has earned the right to a larger pool of titles and status. In the third case, a person has proven herself so valuable that the Grandmothers of the entire nation grant her the recognition and status due to a cultural treasure. To be adopted at the second and third levels is rare, but not unknown, as in the case of the well-loved Harriet Maxwell Converse (1836–1903), adopted at all three levels by the Senecas. Harriet Maxwell Converse, *Myths and Legends of the New York State Iroquois*, in Arthur Caswell Parker (ed.), New York State Museum Bulletin no. 125, Education Department Bulletin no. 437 (Albany: University of the State of New York, 1908), pp. 19, 22, 23.

Bibliography

An Act in Relation to Marriage between White Men and Indian Women, 25 Stat. L., 392, August 9, 1888.

Aupaumut, Hendrick. "A Narrative of an Embassy to the Western Indians," *Memoirs of the Historical Society of Pennsulvania* 2, no. 1 (1827): 9–131.

Barton, Benjamin Smith. *New Views of the Origin of the Tribes and Nations of America* (1798, reprint; Millwood, NY: Kraus Reprint, 1976).

Blauner, Robert. *Racial and Ethnic Groups in America*, 3rd ed. (Dubuque, IA: Kendall Hunt, 1969).

Blumenbach, Johann Friederich. *On the Natural Varieties of Mankind (De Generis Humani Varietate Nativa)* (1795; 1865, reprint; New York: Bergman, 1969).

Board of Indian Commissioners. *Annual Report*, 1885. *House Executive Documents*. 49th Congress, Session I, no. 109 (Washington, DC: Government Printing Office, 1901).

Bolton, Herbert Eugene. *The Rim of Christendom: A Biography of Eusebio Francisco Kino, Pacific Coast Pioneer* (New York: Russell and Russell, 1960).

Bonaparte, Darren. "Running for Safety," *Native Americas* (Winter 2000): 15.

"Bowman's Campaign of 1779," *Ohio Archaeological and Historical Publications* 22 (1913): 502–19.

"Bowman's Expedition against Chillicothe, May–June, 1779," *Ohio Archaeological and Historical Pubilcations* 19 (1910): 446–59.

Brandon, William. The Last Americans: The Indian in American Culture (New York: McGraw-Hill, 1973).

Brodie, Fawn McKay. *No Man Knows My History: The Life of Joseph Smith, The Mormon Prophet*, 2nd ed. (1945; New York: Knopf, 1971).

Marge Bruchac, "Reclaiming the Word 'Squaw' in the Name of the Ancestors," Posted November 1999 on www.nativeweb.org/pages/legal/squaw.html. Accessed December 22, 2005.

Burrage, Henry S., (ed.) *Early English and French Voyages, 1534–1608: Original Narratives of Early American History* (1906; New York: Barnes and Noble, 1967).

Carr, Lucien. "On the Social and Political Position of Woman among the Huron-Iroquois Tribes," Peabody Museum of American Archaeology and Ethnology, Reports 16 and 17, 3.3–4 (1884): 207–32.

Carter, Kent. "Deciding Who Can Be Cherokee: Enrollment Records of the Dawes Commission," *Chronicles of Oklahoma* 69, no. 2 (1991): 174–205.

————. "Federal Indian Policy: Cherokee Enrollment, 1898–1907," *Prologue* 23, no. 1 (1991): 25–31.

Champlain, Samuel de. *The Works of Samuel de Champlain*, Ed. by H. P. Biggar, trans. by W. D. LeSuer and H. H. Langton. 6 vols. (Toronto: Champlain Society, 1936).

Charlevois, Pierre de. *Journal of a Voyage to North America*. 2 vols. (1761; Ann Arbor, MI: University Microfilms, 1966).

Converse, Harriet Maxwell. *Myths and Legends of the New York State Iroquois*, ed. by Arthur Caswell Parker. New York State Museum Bulletin no. 125, Education Department Bulletin no. 437 (Albany: University of the State of New York, 1908).

Cook, Frederick. *Journals of a Military Expedition of Major General John Sullivan against the Six Nations of Indians in 1779* (1887, reprint; Freeport, NY: Books for Libraries, 1972).

Cross, Terry. *Indian Child Welfare Report* (Portland, OR: Indian Child Welfare Association, 2002).

Davis, Nathan. "History of the Expedition against the Five Nations, Commanded by General Sullivan, in 1779," *Historical Magazine* 3, no. 4 (1868): 198–205.

Debo, Angie. *And Still the Waters Run: The Betrayal of the Five Civilized Tribes*, 4th ed. (1940, reprint; Princeton, NJ: Princeton University Press, 1991).

Deloria, Vine Jr. *Custer Died for Your Sins: An Indian Manifesto* (New York: Avon, 1969).

Department of the Interior. *Annual Report to the Commissioner of Indian Affairs for 1895.* 5 vols. (Washington, DC: Government Printing Office, 1896).

Department of the Interior. *Annual Report of the Commissioner of Indian Affairs for the Fiscal Year Ended June 30, 1898* (Washington, DC: Government Printing Office, 1898).

Department of the Interior. *Annual Report of the Commissioner of Indian Affairs for the Fiscal Year Ended June 30, 1905.* Part 1 (Washington, DC: Government Printing Office, 1906).

Donnelly, Ignatius. *Atlantis: The Antediluvian World*, ed. by Egerton Sykes (1881; New York: Harper and Brothers, 1949).

Dowd, Gregory Evans. *A Spirited Resistance: North American Indian Struggle for Unity, 1745–1815* (Baltimore: Johns Hopkins University Press, 1992).

Drinnon, Richard. *Facing West: The Metaphysics of Indian-Hating and Empire-Building.* (Minneapolis: University of Minnesota Press, 1980).

The Eastern Band of Cherokees v. The United States and the Cherokee Nation, 20 Ct. Cl. 449, 479 (1885), in *Cases Decided in the Court of Claims at the Term of 1884–'85*, vol. 20 (Washington, DC: Government Printing Office, 1885), pp. 449–83.

Eastern Band of Cherokee Indians v. United States and Cherokee Nation, Commonly Called Cherokee Nation West, 117 U.S. 288 (1885), in *United States Reports*, vol. 117, *Cases Adjudged in The Supreme Court at October Term 1885* (New York: Banks and Brothers, Law Publishers, 1886), pp. 288–313.

Fawcett, Melissa Jayne [Tantaquidgeon]. *The Lasting of the Mohegans, Part I: The Story of the Wolf People* (Uncasville, CT: The Mohegan Tribe, 1995).

Fenton, William N. (ed.). *Parker on the Iroquois* (New York: Syracuse University Press, 1968).

Filson, John. *The Discovery and Settlement of Kentucke.* (1784, reprint; Ann Arbor, MI: University Microfilms, 1966).

Forbes, Jack D. *Africans and Native Americans: The Language of Race and the Evolution of Red-Black Peoples* (Urbana: University of Illinois Press, 1993).

Foreman, Grant. *The Five Civilized Tribes* (Norman: University of Oklahoma Press, 1934).

Fox, Robin. *Kinship and Marriage* (Baltimore: Penguin Books, 1967).

Franklin, Benjamin. *Writings* (New York: Library of America, 1987).

Galloway, Patricia. *Choctaw Genesis, 1500–1700* (Lincoln: University of Nebraska Press, 1995).

Galton, Francis. *English Men of Science: Their Nature and Nurture* (New York: D. Appleton, 1875).

————. *Hereditary Genius: An Inquiry into Its Laws and Consequences* (1869; New York: D. Appleton, 1884).

————. *Inquiries into Human Faculty and Its Development* (1883; London: J. M. Den, 1907).

————. *Natural Inheritance* (1889, reprint; New York: AMS Press, 1973).

"The Gourd Dance." Wyandotte Nation of Oklahoma Web site at www.wyandotte-nation.org/community/the_dances.html. Posted November 1, 2005, accessed November 30, 2005.

Government Accounting Office. "The BIA's Tribal Trust Fund Account Reconciliation Results," Report number GAO/AIMD–96–93. Report to the Committee on Indian Affairs, U.S. Senate. May 3, 1996.

Green, Rayna. "A Tribe Called Wannabee: Playing Indian in America and Europe," *Folklore* 9, no. 1 (1988): 30–55.

Greenfield, Lawrence, and Steven Smith. *American Indians and Crime.* U.S. Department of Justice, Office of Justice Programs. (Washington, DC: Bureau of Justice Statistics Clearinghouse, 1999).

Harjo, Joy. "Identity: Part Deux," *Indian Country Today*. Posted online at www.indiancountry.com/content.cfm?id=1096410704 on April 7, 2005; accessed June 9, 2005.

Heckewelder, John. *History, Manners, and Customs of the Indian Nations Who Once Inhabited Pennsylvania and the Neighboring States*. First American Frontier Series (1820; 1876, reprint; New York: Arno Press and *The New York Times*, 1971).

Jacobs, Renee. "Iroquois Great Law of Peace and the United States Constitution: How the Founding Fathers Ignored the Clan Mothers," Notes, *American Indian Law Review* 16, no. 2 (1991): 497–531.

Jennings, Jennifer, and Charon Asetoyer. "The Impact of AIDS in the Native American Community" (Lake Andes, SD: Native American Women's Health Center, 1996).

Johansen, Bruce E. "The New York Oneidas: A Business Called a Nation," in Bruce E. Johansen (ed.), *Enduring Legacies: Native American Treaties and Contemporary Controversies* (Westport, CT: Praeger, 2004), pp. 95–133.

Joseph, Rachel. "Indian Health Care Improvement Act Reauthorization Amendments of 2004," hearing on SB 212/ HR 2440 before the House Resources Committee, 107th Congress. Testimony of Rachel Joseph, Cochair, National Steering Committee, 2004.

Kehoe, Alice Beck. *North American Indians: A Comprehensive Account*, 2nd ed. (Englewood Cliffs, NJ: Prentice Hall, 1992), p. 203.

Kidwell, Clara Sue. *Choctaws and Missionaries in Mississippi, 1818–1918* (Norman: University of Oklahoma Press, 1995).

Lafitau, Joseph François. *Customs of the American Indians Compared with the Customs of Primitive Times*, ed. and trans. by William N. Fenton and Elizabeth L. Moore. 2 vols. (1724; Toronto: Champlain Society, 1974).

Lassiter, Luke E. *The Power of Kiowa Song: A Collaborative Ethnography*. Posted online at www.uapress.arizona.edu/extras/kiowa/kiowasng.htm, October 4, 1998, accessed December 4, 2005.

Lewis, Ron, and M. K. Ho, "Social Work with Native Americans," *Social Work* (Sept. 1975): 379–82.

Mann, Barbara Alice. "Euro-Forming the Data," in Bruce E. Johansen, *Debating Democracy: Native American Legacy of Freedom* (Santa Fe: Clear Light, 1998), pp. 178–80.

———. *George Washington's War on Native America* (Westport, CT: Praeger, 2005).

———. "The Greenville Treaty of 1795: Pen-and-Ink Witchcraft in the Struggle for the Old Northwest" in Bruce E. Johansen (ed.), *Enduring Legacies: Native American Treaties and Contemporary Controversies* (Westport, CT: Praeger, 2004), pp. 136–201.

———. "Haudenosaunee (Iroquois) Women, Legal and Political Status," in Bruce Elliott Johansen (ed.), *The Encyclopedia of Native American Legal Tradition* (Westport, CT: Greenwood, 1998), pp. 112–31.

———. *Iroquoian Women: The Gantowisas* (New York: Lang, 2004).

———. "'A Man of Misery': Chitto Harjo and the Senate Select Committee on Oklahoma Statehood," in Barbara Alice Mann (ed.), *Native American Speakers of the Eastern Woodlands: Selected Speeches and Critical Analyses* (Westport, CT: Greenwood, 2001), pp. 197–228.

———. *Native Americans, Archaeologists, and the Mounds* (New York: Peter Lang, 2003).

———, and Jerry L. Fields, "A Sign in the Sky: Dating the League of the Haudenosaunee," *American Indian Culture and Research Journal* 21, no. 2 (1997): 105–63.

[McKee, Alexander.] *Minutes of Debates in Council on the Banks of the Ottawa River, (Commonly Called the Miami of the Lake), November, 1791* (Philadelphia: William Young, Bookseller, 1792).

McNickle, D'Arcy. *The Surrounded* (New York: Dodd, Mead and Co., 1936).

Montoya v. United States, 180 U.S., 261 (1901); 21 S. Ct., 358, 359 (190), in National Reporter System, *The Supreme Court Reporter, November, 1900–July, 1901,* vol. 21 (St. Paul, MN: West Publishing, 1901).

Oswalt, Wendell H. *This Land Was Theirs: A Study of the North American Indian* (New York: Wiley, 1966).

Parker, Arthur C[aswell] [*Gawaso Waneh*]. *An Analytical History of the Seneca Indians.* Researches and Transactions of the New York State

Archaeological Association, Lewis H. Morgan Chapter (1926, reprint; New York: Kraus Reprint., 1970).

———. *The Constitution of the Five Nations, or the Iroquois Book of the Great Law* (Albany: University of the State of New York, 1916).

———. "The Maize Maiden," in *Rumbling Wings and Other Indian Tales* (Garden City, NY: Doubleday, Doran and Company, 1928), pp. 179–91.

Pasternak, Burton. *Introduction to Kinship and Social Organization* (Englewood Cliffs, NJ: Prentice Hall, 1976).

Prucha, Francis Paul. *The Great Father: The United States Government and the American Indians.* 2 vols. (Lincoln: University of Nebraska Press, 1984).

Reed, Marcelina. *Seven Clans of the Cherokee* (Cherokee, NC: Cherokee Publications, 1993).

Rosen, Kenneth (ed.). *The Man to Send Rain Clouds: Contemporary Stories by American Indians* (New York: Vintage Books, 1975).

Rupert, Ross A. *Dancing With a Ghost: Exploring Indian Reality* (Toronto: Reed Books, 1992).

Sagard, Gabriel. *The Long Journey to the Country of the Hurons*, trans. by H. H. Langton (1632; Toronto: Champlain Society, 1939).

Schuler, Margaret. "Women and the Law," in R.S. Gallin, M. Aronoff, and A. Ferguson (eds.), *Women and International Development*, Annual vol. 1 (Boulder, CO: Westview: 1986), pp. 155–187.

Silverberg, Robert. *Mound Builders of Ancient America: The Archaeology of a Myth* (Greenwich, CT: New York Graphic Society, 1968).

Smith, Ethan. *View of the Hebrews; Exhibiting the Destruction of Jerusalem; the Certain Restoration of Judah and Israel; the Present State of Judah and Israel; and an Address of the Prophet Isaiahy Relative to their Restoration* (Poultney, VT: Smith and Shurte, 1823).

Smith, J. David. *The Eugenic Assault on America: Scenes in Red, White, and Black* (Fairfax, VA: George Mason University Press, 1993).

Spaulding, Solomon. *The "Manuscript Found" or "Manuscript Story," of the Late Rev. Solomon Spaulding from a Verbatim Copy of the Original Now in the Care of Pres. James H. Fiarchild of Oberlin College, Ohio* (Lamoni, IA: Reorganized Church, 1885).

Steele, Ian K. *Warpaths: Invasions of North America* (New York: Oxford University Press, 1994).

Thornton Russell. "Cherokee Population Losses During the Trail of Tears: A New Perspective and a New Estimate," *Ethnohistory* 31 (1984): 289–300.

Thwaites, Rueben Gold (ed. and trans.). *The Jesuit Relations: Travels and Explorations of the Jesuit Missionaries in New France, 1610–1791.* 73 vols. (New York: Pageant Book, 1959).

Torphy, Sally S. "Native American Women and Coerced Sterilization: On the Trail of Tears in the 1970's," *American Indian Cultures and Research Journal* 24, no. 2 (2000): 1–22.

U.S. Census Bureau. "Poverty in the United States: 2001: Current Population Reports" (Washington, DC: Government Printing Office, 2002).

U.S. Census Bureau. *Employment Status 2000: Census Brief.* Available online at www.census.gov/prod/2003pubs/c2kbr-18.pdf.

U.S. Commission on Civil Rights, Testimony of Rachel A. Joseph, cochair National Steering Committee, *Broken Promises 2004. Evaluating the Native America Health Care System Reauthorization of the Indian Health Care Improvement Act*; hearing on SB 212 and HR 2440 before Senate Committee on Indian Affairs and House Resources Committee, 107th Congress.

U.S. Department of Justice, Bureau of Statistics. *American Indians and Crime* (Washington DC: BJS Clearinghouse, 2004).

U.S. Department of Labor, Bureau of Indian Affairs. *1995 Annual Report, Quiet Crisis: Federal Funding and Un-met Needs in Indian Country* (Washington, DC: Government Printing Office, 2003).

van der Donck, Adriaen Cornelissen. "Description of New Netherland," 1653. in Dean Snow, Charles T. Gehring, and William A. Starna (eds.), *In Mohawk Country: Early Narrative about a Native People*, trans. by Diederick Goedhuys (Syracuse: Syracuse University Press, 1996), pp. 104–30.

Vander Wall, Jim. "American Indian Women at the Center of the Indigenous Resistance in Contemporary North America," in M. Annette

Jaimes (ed.), *The State of Native America: Genocide, Colonization and Resistance* (Boston: South End Press, 1992), pp. 311–44.

Van Doren, Mark (ed.). *The Travels of William Bartram* (1791; New York: Dover, 1955).

Wall, Steve. *Wisdom's Daughters: Conversations with Women Elders of Native America* (New York: Harper Perennial, 1993).

Webster, Noah. "Antiquity: Letter III. From Mr. N. Webster, to the Rev. Dr. Stiles, President of Yale College, on the Remains of the Fortifications in the Western Country. Dated New-York January 20, 1788," *American Magazine* (February 1788): 146–56.

White, Richard. *The Middle Ground: Indians, Empires, and Republics, in the Great Lakes Region, 1650–1815* (New York: Cambridge University Press, 1991).

Williams, S. C. (ed.). *Lieutenant Henry Timberlake's Memoirs, 1756–1765* (1927, reprint; Marietta, GA: Continental Book Company, 1948).

Wright, J. Leitch. *The Only Land They Knew: The Tragic Story of the American Indians in the Old South* (New York: Free Press, 1981).

Winsor, Justin (ed.). *Narrative and Critical History of America.* 8 vols. (Boston: Houghton, Mifflin and Co., 1884–1889).

Wright, Albert Hazen. *The Sullivan Expedition of 1779: Contemporary Newspaper Comment.* Studies in History, nos. 5, 6, 7, and 8, 4 parts. (Ithaca, NY: A. H. Wright, 1943).

Contributors' Biographies

~

PAULA GUNN ALLEN, Laguna/Metis, is a Ph.D. Professor Emerita, UCLA. Her anthologies of critical studies and American Indian fiction include *Studies in American Indian Literature* (1983), *Spider Woman's Granddaughters: Traditional Tales and Contemporary Writing by American Indian Women* (1989), and two collections of her essays, *The Sacred Hoop: Recovering the Feminine in American Indian Traditions* (1986), *and Off the Reservation: Reflections on Boundary Busting, Border-Crossing, Loose Canons* (1998), several poetry books, including *Life Is A Fatal Disease* (1998); and a novel, *The Woman Who Owned the Shadows* (1982). Her essays, poetry and fiction have appeared in a number of collections and journals, including, *The American Scholar, Blue Mesa, Zyzziva, Shenandoah, A Circle of Nations: Voices and Visions of American Indians*, ed. John G attuso, *Weaving the Visions*, ed Judith Plaskow and Charol Christ, *Eyes of the Deer*, ed. Carolyn Dunn Anderson, *Speaking the Enemy's Language*, ed. Joy Harjo. Gunn Allen has won a number of awards, including the Hubbell Medal for Lifetime Achievement, The Modern Language Association of America, (2000) and Native Writer's Circle Lifetime Achievement Award (2001). Her biography of Pocahontas, *Pocahontas: Medicine Woman, Spy, Entrepreneur, in Diplomat*, was published by Harper San Francisco, October 2003. Presently she is working on her memoirs, *Wayward Spirit*, and a volume of poetry, *America the Beautiful*.

LEE MARACLE, Sto:Loh nation, grandmother of four, mother of four, was born in North Vancouver, B. C. and now resides in Innisfil, Ontario. Her works include: the novels, *Ravensong* (1993), *Bobbi Lee* (1990), *Sundogs* (1992); short story collection, *Sojourner's Truth* (1990); poetry collection, *Bentbox* (2000), and the non-fiction work, *I Am Woman* (1996). Maracle is co-editor of *My Home As I Remember* (2000) and *Telling It: Women and Language Across Cultures* (1990); editor of a number of poetry works and the *Gatherings* journals; and has published in dozens of anthologies in Canada and America. Maracle is a both an award-winning author and teacher. She currently is Mentor For Aboriginal Students at University of Toronto where she also is a teacher and the Traditional Cultural Director for the Indigenous Theatre School, where she is a part-time cultural instructor.

[Bettie] KAY GIVENS MCGOWAN is of Choctaw, Cherokee, and Irish descent. Born in Mississippi, she is a cultural anthropologist who received her undergraduate degrees from the University of Michigan at Dearborn and her Ph.D. in 1994, from Wayne State University. Today, she teaches Anthropology and Native American Studies and Racial and Ethnic Studies at Eastern Michigan University, in Ypsilanti, and Marygrove College, in Detroit.

BARBARA ALICE MANN, of Seneca descent, is a Ph.D. scholar working in Native American Studies. As a faculty member at the University of Toledo, she has authored several books, including, *George Washington's War on Native America* (2005), *Native Americans, Archaeologists, and the Mounds* (2004), and *Iroquoian Women: The Gantowisas* (2004), as well as co-authored *Encyclopedia of the Haudenosaunee* (2000) and *Debating Democracy* (1998). In addition, she has published numerous chapters, particularly "The Greenville Treaty of 1795: Pen-and-Ink Witchcraft in the Struggle for the Old Northwest" in *Enduring Legacies: Native American Treaties and Contemporary Controversies* (2004). Her articles include, "'Your Portion Is Unhappily So Small: Jane Austen and the Dreadful Proposal,'" in *Persuasions* (2003); "In Defense of the Ancestors," in *Native Americas* (2000), "The Lynx in Time: Haudenosaunee

Women's Traditions and History" in *American Indian Quarterly* (1997); "A Sign in the Sky: Dating the League of the Haudenosaunee" in *American Indian Culture and Research Journal* (1997); and "The Fire at Onondaga: Wampum as Proto-Writing," (1995). She lives, writes, teaches, and works for indigenous causes in her home state of Ohio.

Index